Dear Reader ▮

I hope my journey helps you with your own. You might even feel like giving up but the universe won't let you. I know you will come out stronger than when you first started this and when you do, I'd love to connect with you on your experiences.

A Sacred Journey

The Road to Rediscovering My

Spirituality

Andrea Anne Aloysius

Copyright © 2022 Andrea Anne Aloysius
ISBN: 978-1-945642-15-9
This book is licensed for your personal enjoyment only. This book may not be re-sold or given away to other people. If you would like to share this book with another person, please purchase an additional copy for each recipient. If you're reading this book and did not purchase it, or it was not purchased for your use only, then please return to your favorite book retailer and purchase your own copy. Thank you for respecting the hard work of this author.
All rights reserved.

Table of Contents

- Acknowledgments 7
- Dedications 9
- **Introduction** 10
- **Not A Ghost Story** 16
- **My Childhood** 23
- **Reiki To The Rescue** 28
- **Meditations, Manifestations & Reading People** 34
- Life Beyond Reiki 42
- Discovering Astral Travel 49
- **The Seven-Year Glitch** 53
- **Finding My Way Home to Reiki** 58
- **Double, Double, Toil & Trouble – I Was In Trouble** 69
- **Double, Double, Toil & Trouble – Reclaiming What's Mine** 79
- **Enhancing My Abilities – The Akashic Records & Channeling** 85
- **My Spiritual Growth Spurt** 98
- **All About Meditation** 103
- **Spirit Guides** 115
- **Conversations with My Higher Self** 119
- **My Daily Practices** 129
- **Find Your Own Groove** 143
- **Conclusion** 150
- **About the Author** 154
- Connect with Andrea 156

Acknowledgments

I would like to thank all the divinities who assisted me through writing this book and for making sure I followed through.

Thank you, Mummy, for forcing me to go for my first ever Reiki session. Because of you and your influence, I embarked on this amazing journey. I love you.

Thank you, Aish, for the support and encouragement. Thank you for all the readings you did for me even when you were annoyed at me. I love you.

Thank you, Marcus, for giving me my space whenever I have needed it with unconditional love, smiles and food, especially ice cream. You are the best husband for me and I love you more than I can ever express.

Thank you, Acha, for having shared your ghost stories with me and for occasionally acknowledging that there is "something" in the area when you see it. I love you.

Thank you, Ammumma, for never judging me no matter what I did and for sharing with me your experiences post WWII about the hauntings which Appuppa was never able to witness. I love you and miss you very much.

Thank you, Fiona, my favorite puppy in America for always letting me know that there are uninvited "visitors" that we need to send off. You are my favorite and only child and I love you very much.

To all of my masters, teachers, and mentors, thank you for your guidance since 2006. I will soldier on my spiritual journey!

Thank you to Jiewei (Piggy) and Huiling (Girl Girl aka GerGer) who have been my pillars of strength for over half my life even though I am far away from you. Thank you for the fun and laughter and for all the support you've given me since 2006. I love you both immensely.

Thank you to everyone who has ever allowed me to either perform a healing session on you or do a reading for you and to teach you what I have learnt. Your feedback has helped make me a better reader and healer.

Dedications

To everyone who has walked off the beaten path, completely lost your way like me and is slowly rediscovering your spirituality as I have. You are not alone.

To anyone who has struggled with the ability to talk about what might be considered taboo subjects in your home, meditation, or any spiritual aspect in your lives, I hope this book gives you the confidence, courage and strength to weather the storm.

There is always a rainbow after a storm.

Introduction

"I see dead people."

Do you remember this famous line from the movie, The Sixth Sense? Unlike him, I do not see dead people, but hear them and feel them all the time, and have for my whole life. This book isn't a ghost story, but that doesn't mean there are no ghosts involved. As soon as I realized I could sense them, ghosts and spirits have communicated with me. Obviously, it was difficult to deal with this during my younger days but later on, I would learn how to help send them to the light. If we can talk to or see otherworldly beings, we are called mediums or psychic mediums. Those terminologies never made sense to me until very recently. Heck, I had no knowledge of being a medium. Or a psychic for the matter!

My spiritual journey may have started since my birth, I don't know. My spiritual side, however, started through Reiki, not ghosts. Actually, my mother inadvertently played a part in this because she forced me to go for my first ever Reiki session. Not knowing what it was or what it would do, I kept returning for more sessions and eventually studied all three levels of Usui Reiki.

Practicing Reiki helped me deal with my anger issues and improve my level of patience. It helped me become a better person and more fun for people to be around me. Growing with Reiki was an eye-opener. Learning to psychically read people, see their auras and finally be able to help these lingering spirits go into the light gave me great joy. Meditation also became the paramount of my life. Prior to Reiki, meditation was non-existent.

Through meditation, I learnt how to communicate with the divinities – gods and goddesses, angels, the universe. This was something that I had been doing for my entire life but never talked about at home, just like ghosts.

Volunteering at the Reiki Center regularly aided my spiritual growth. Once it closed down, I was introduced to an Egyptian healing center where I experienced magic and power like no other. For about seven years, right at the peak of my spiritual life, I uprooted my life in Singapore and immigrated to the U.S. Great! That was my lifelong dream anyway, so leaving home and moving to the U.S. made sense to me!

The side effect of relocation was falling off the bandwagon and totally losing touch with my spiritual side. My entire support system was at home, in Singapore – my mother and my sister. Without them, short of feeling lost, unmotivated and completely uninterested in continuing with all that was accomplished in the last seven years, my practices faded. I did not intentionally give up; I honestly didn't! The thing is the three of us did this together all the time. It was more of a family thing, and since my family wasn't physically here with me, even sitting down to meditate was painfully difficult. By the way, meditation had always made me cringe; I very strongly disliked it!

The lack of practicing meditation caused me to fall into a downward spiral, and the distance between my spirituality and me only grew wider. For the next seven years, despite being in many difficult situations, my spirituality didn't forsake me, not once. I did not give up on it either. Even though actively practicing had ceased, my spiritual gifts were always within me and I was aware of what needed to be done to get these reactivated. This is what many of us do – we pray only when we really need help or want something. But how many of us actually give thanks after we have received the help we've asked for? That was my predicament during my seven-year hiatus as well. There were times that asking for help was more the norm for me than thanking the universe for having given it to me. So you see what I meant when I said I didn't give up on my spirituality and I wasn't forsaken either? The divinities were always with me when I needed them and I knew it too. Soon enough, I would need them more than I had ever needed them in my entire life.

My spirituality came back to me at the utmost crucial moment in my life. The universe knows what you need when you need it and it'll give it to you. It starts in small doses and if you pay enough attention, you'll know to prepare yourself for it. There are times that you may have disregarded these signs as I did because you thought they were insignificant. Then, it hits you, like an avalanche or a boulder coming at you, and you don't even have time to react anymore!

This book depicts my entire spiritual journey thus far, right from the beginning of Reiki, through how I completely lost touch with everything spiritual and the mainspring of my comeback. In the upcoming chapters, you will read about some of my childhood experiences, my current spiritual practices and even share some of the techniques I have picked up along the way. If you have trod down a similar path to mine and are amidst finding your way back, hopefully my journey gives you the motivation and strength to persevere in a way that I was never able to in those seven years. Everyone's path is different, but with a little help from our support system, we can all reach our ultimate destinations and find our happy places. Even if you haven't lost your way, this book can still be a guide to help you with the meditation techniques and visualization skills you have difficulties with, amongst other tidbits! Let's all do this together!

Not A Ghost Story

As I sat in the bedroom where my so-called study table was doing my homework after school that sunny Tuesday afternoon, I heard someone calling my name.

"Andrea."

The door was closed; my name sounded like a whisper. I remember turning my head around to see who it was because the sound came from behind me.

There was nobody.

Perhaps it was my maternal grandmother or maybe our maid calling for me from the kitchen. My newborn baby sister was rocking in her cradle in the living room, which made me think they would not shout as they would not want to wake the sleeping baby up. However, wanting to complete my studying and homework for the day quickly to be able to play, mixed with being too lazy to leave the bedroom, I shouted back in my mother tongue, Malayalam,

"What?"

There was no response. Thinking that perhaps they did not need me anymore, I continued with my mundane task of toughing it out and reading my Primary Three (third grade) Science textbook.

"Andrea!"

It was so soft but still loud enough for me to hear it. Again, since the voice came from behind me, my automatic reaction was to turn my head around. There was still no one. Thinking that it was my grandmother again, this time, opening the door and stepping out of the bedroom, without even thinking about my sister who was sound asleep, I shouted even louder to get their attention since they didn't hear me the first time. The two women got taken aback because they both came running out of the kitchen with perplexed looks on their faces and asked me what I meant by "what?"

It all became so confusing. Attributing this strange phenomenon to my wild imagination and thinking, I stared blankly at my textbook instead of reading the words. It was difficult to focus. I must have reread the same sentence over a dozen times because nothing registered in my brain. This time, a few minutes went by before I heard this ostentatious sound so loudly and unmistakably in my left ear as if somebody was standing right next to me. "ANDREA!

Startled by the loud voice, to the point of jumping out of my seat and almost out of my skin because I felt breath on my left ear. I turned around and screamed to match the tone of the voice.

"WHAT?!"

However, there was no one in the room. Nine year old me, freaked out completely and ran into the kitchen telling my grandmother what had just happened.

I have no recollection of what transpired afterwards but it did leave a lasting impact. I wrote about this incident time after time in my school essays, but changed one crucial part. The endings always said I finally woke up from a dream, and it just fell flat. All of my teachers hated it, even though they loved the story. There was no possibility of me taking a chance and telling them the truth, what if they didn't believe it? Every time this story was recounted, I got goosebumps. This might sound like a ghost story now, but I promise it isn't!

Throughout my life, my mother told people many stories about how I would see things or talk to those very things as a child. Strangely, I had no recollection of any of those occurrences before the age of nine when the incident above took place. That was most certainly my earliest memory of experiencing anything even remotely close to what I would end up facing when I embraced my spirituality in the coming years. Sometimes, regardless of the time of day, things would somehow follow me home on my way back from school or my extra-curricular activities. This continued into my mid-teens. They would typically go away after some time which made me think nothing of it. They never talked to me. At least, I didn't think they did. I couldn't hear them at all, so even if they attempted to talk to me, there was no way for me to have known. I was also unable to see them. All I know is that I could always feel them and distinctly knew that sometimes they followed me home. Nobody in my house ever spoke about ghosts or being able to see them or communicate with them. Therefore, communication with spirits never crossed my mind. Nor did the idea to discuss these situations with anyone.

Eventually, my ability to sense these things stopped, or went on a pause even though somehow I was well aware of their existence.

Well, perhaps "stopped sensing them" is an inaccurate and incorrect statement. Instead, it's more accurate to say that I did my best not to pay heed to them. Please forgive me for choosing not to pay them any attention. It was getting a tad bit annoying. This was something that was constantly in the back of my mind and as much as the thought of escaping from this was so tempting at times, I couldn't. Even when they deliberately made their presence known to me, I would just as deliberately block them out to avoid dealing with them. I did not enjoy dealing with ghosts. That was it. I was a child who did not want to converse with or have anything to do with ghosts. Practically throughout my entire childhood and adolescence, I prayed that they would leave me alone but sadly, that never happened.

It is strange to reminisce about this now, but my grandmother always told us horror stories about how she was attacked at night by ghosts, and my grandfather, who was sleeping right next to her, could not see her struggling or hear her screaming her lungs out. She mentioned frantically waving her arms in the air and hitting him in her attempts to wake him up, but he neither felt nor heard anything. On the other hand, my father would tell us stories he had encountered whilst working at a cemetery when he was young. He also told us about other stories during his military days when he was older. These two people, my maternal grandmother and my father, would tell us such stories, so somehow, their bloodline would have inherited these traits as well, correct? Absolutely! There is no doubt that I got my gifts from both sides, and it seemed like all these "gifts" amplified for me. All these stories that I had heard growing up were their experiences. Nothing was ever discussed in-depth and therefore, no questions were asked. They'd tell me their stories and move on to the next thing. No one discussed this at home so I never paid attention to how these gifts would be helpful to me later on in my life. Did I already mention that this is not a ghost story?

My Childhood

Before I can go into the essence of what this book is about, you need to understand a bit about my background and upbringing. I was born and grew up in Singapore to a Malayalee-Hindu mother and a Tamil-Roman Catholic father. To keep things simple, they are both ethnically Indian but different kinds of Indians; they were also born and raised in Singapore just as I was, and they were both raised with different religious backgrounds. Simple enough, right?

Growing up in a multi-religious household gave me lots of perspective on the two main religions we practiced at home – Roman Catholicism and Hinduism. Following the Catholic faith, my parents got me baptized as a child, therefore, growing up, I went to church and attended Catechism classes. Simultaneously, I also followed the Hindu faith going to the temple with my mother. Many things they taught me at church boggled my mind, especially about the deities from various religions being at loggerheads with each other. That made no bloody sense to me at all! I mean, I talked to Jesus and Mother Mary, Ganesha and a bunch of other Hindu divinities and none of them ever yelled at me or judged me for praying to the other. Sometimes, they would all be in the same room with me and we would all communicate with each other. During my childhood, my nightly ritual was to pray before falling asleep. My prayers consisted of full-on conversations with Jesus before sleeping, and I swear we conversed with each other like we were long-time friends. That was how it was at the church and at the temple too. I talked to the divinities as though they were my friends and remembered them fervently responding to me. All of this could not possibly have just been in my head!

My father has been a relatively staunch Roman Catholic his whole life. He never imposed his views on others and did not concern himself with anyone else's religious or spiritual beliefs. He stuck with Jesus, Mother Mary and the Holy Spirit. My mother, on the other hand, as much of a devout Hindu as she was and still is, prayed to everyone. If she needed help with something and knew of divinities or deities from other religions that could potentially help her with her cause, she would pray to them and ask them for help. There was no discrimination there, and there is no shame in admitting that I took after her in that sense. In fact, I truly am proud of inheriting this trait from her. She would go to church and attend Mass and Novena and also do poojas or prayers at the temple. We always had a prayer room in our house and an altar where all the deities were together. With the exception of my father, the rest of us prayed to not just Jesus and Mother Mary, but to all the Hindu gods and goddesses that hung on the walls or sat on the dresser of the prayer room in our house as well. Because of the influence I had, I grew up believing in and praying to both sides. This is something I am eternally grateful for because being multi-religious has helped me easily embrace all things spiritual and not be religious, if that makes sense.

Today, my mother's house feels like an amalgamated place of worship that consists of all the various divinities from all the religions that exist. She was the one who introduced my family to Reiki and meditation through the Reiki center that she forced me to visit. I can say that she forced me now because it truly was the stepping-stone to my spiritual transformation, and also, it is the hard truth; she did indeed force me. She won't admit to it so don't ask her! My father would soon go for healing sessions too, but he never studied the healing art form.

As much as the Catholic Church teachings told me otherwise, there was never an internal conflict about whom I should or should not be praying to. Having always been able to directly connect with the divinities ever since I was a child enabled me to see that being multi-religious was seriously a non-issue. The divinities themselves didn't have conflicts with me swinging both ways, so it certainly didn't matter what anyone else thought. Having had this natural flare was the catalyst that enabled me to connect with other divinities that I had not worked with before, such as the ancient Egyptian divinities and other beings of light, which I will go into further detail in later chapters. Typically, when someone is drawn to Egypt, it is usually because they have had at least one past life there. I have had multiple past lives there, and I found this out through meditation over a few days and through astral traveling. Of course, the divinities guided me through it all. We will discuss meditation and astral traveling in many of the later chapters as well.

Reiki To The Rescue

What I am about to reveal might be unbelievable to anyone who has gotten to know me in the more recent years, so brace yourselves for an honest-to-god (and goddess) truth. I was an angry child. Oh my goodness, I was terrible! As a teenager, I was *much* worse. I got angry at the drop of a hat. I screamed and shouted at anyone and everyone in these moments of anger, with no regard to who the person was and sometimes, with no regard to where I was at either. My family usually bore the brunt of it all.

When I was 18, my sister was diagnosed with dyslexia. She was about eight or nine at the time. She couldn't study well and had a short attention span when it came to concentrating on pretty much anything, specifically, her studies. As a result, her grades were terrible. Her teachers and my family not only scolded her but also constantly punished her for this. A friend of my mother's told her about this Reiki center that helped her autistic child. Not knowing anything about Reiki and with the sole intention of helping my sister get better, my mother started taking my sister to this Reiki center for Reiki sessions.

When my mother saw that Reiki helped my sister, she asked me – well, more like told me – to go to this Reiki center for a session of my own. Why? I mean, I didn't have issues like my sister had. What the hell is Reiki and what was it going to help me with? She responded with a simple two-worded answer. That was the method she used to get me to do her bidding - be it to go somewhere or do something that I simply didn't want to do. It was her go-to method when I asked way too many questions about those very things that I was just reluctant to do, "Just go; Sheesh! Well, okay then! I begrudgingly obliged. As an Asian girl, it was expected of me to listen to my mother or be prepared to face her wrath. She would somehow find a way to ignore me for a few days and guilt trips were a huge part of my heritage. You could even call it emotional blackmail of sorts. Despite the deafening, deadly silence that would have reared its ugly head had I refused to abide by this, I would have eventually caved in any way just to make her happy. Don't ask her about this either because she will deny it! Therefore, before she could get mad at me, I very reluctantly went for my first ever Reiki session.

Let me admit that it was rather confusing initially. My first ever Reiki session filled me with bouts of confusion. First of all, I did not know what to expect because no one explained anything to me. Secondly, I did not feel anything during my session. When I arrived at the Reiki center, this lady greeted me and took me to a dimly lit room where she asked me to lie down on a massage bed. Later on, I found out that she was a Reiki practitioner. Then, she touched me in what I thought were weird places without providing me with an explanation of what she was going to do or what would be happening to me. It was the most bizarre thing I had ever experienced, and I felt very uncomfortable about this entire situation. Nonetheless, I fell asleep listening to some soothing music with chimes. Come to think of it, the fact that I fell asleep could probably be why I didn't feel anything. It was a shock to my system when the Reiki practitioner woke me up from my sweet slumber. How embarrassing! Honestly, the sleep was just what I needed. Since falling asleep was an issue, going for more sessions seemed like a great idea and I willingly went on my own after that. My mother no longer had to force me. Little did I know what Reiki was doing to me and that this was truly the start of my spiritual growth.

The Reiki center also held meditations. We would go as a family - as in, my mother, sister and I - and meditate with the group. Meditation was a foreign concept to me before the Reiki center. It was not something I even attempted to do prior and did not know what it entailed. The images that came to mind when I thought of meditation were of the saints and sages who lived in the mountains and the monks in monasteries. I pictured them sitting on rocks or on mountaintops with their eyes closed, in silence with so much discipline. There was no bloody way I could ever do that - I had no discipline! Or so I thought. Obviously now I know that they aren't the only ones who meditated. I recall one day, while both my mother and I were there, the Reiki Master asked her about how I was doing. She took a look at me and without any hesitation whatsoever responded to him,

"Her anger has subsided a lot. She is much calmer and is less temperamental now. She does not get angry at the drop of a hat as often as she used to."

She might have also added that I was much happier and smiled more. It has been so long I am unable to remember verbatim. Regardless, her words caught me by surprise because I did not see any changes within myself at all. Everyone else seemed to have noticed the changes in me so Reiki was most certainly doing its thing, whatever that thing was. Although I did not notice the changes within myself, I did notice the subtle differences in my sister. She was able to focus more on her studies and was able to concentrate for prolonged periods. Her attention span grew more than it had ever in all her nine years of age. Her grades started to improve as well. If Reiki was working for her, I was sure it was working for me and I started believing that it was.

Meditations, Manifestations & Reading People

My mother and I eventually took Reiki levels one and two together in that same year and shortly after, I also took up the Reiki Master level course. Constantly volunteering at the Reiki center really helped me to grow my spiritual abilities. Consistency was the key to my development, something I understood very quickly. Here, I learnt about manifestations and reading people for the first time. Let's discuss manifestations first. I learnt that I could ask for anything I wanted and the universe would grant it to me. It was crazy to think something like that could ever happen but what was even crazier was that it actually did! My goodness, it happened! Who would have ever thought that everything you had ever wanted could be yours just by thinking about it? It takes a lot of practice and perseverance, unlearning, even some reprogramming of many things that you were taught to believe your entire life. Regardless, you can make it happen!

You have heard the saying "seek and ye shall find, ask and ye shall receive," right? That is precisely what manifesting is. You are putting your desires out to the universe and asking for the universe to give them to you, a granting of wishes. During one of our meditation sessions one day, I remember that all of us in the group decided that we would be manifesting for a four-digit number to strike first prize. It is kind of like playing the lottery, but you picked four individual numbers of your liking to play this. We felt that this was a very simple thing to envision during our sessions and unanimously voted on a specific four-digit number. We manifested this specific number combination winning the first prize for a few weeks and many of us bought tickets weekly. The first few times that the numbers came out, they were out of order. Still, some of us won a little money. A few weeks later, those who continued buying the tickets won the second prize because the combination that came out that particular week was the same sequence that we had been manifesting for about two months or so! Brilliant is it not? I don't know if anyone ever won the first prize for that number combination, but when some of us won money for the numbers coming out as second prize, we were ecstatic! Remember, you manifest while you meditate. Manifestations, check. Meditations, check.

How exactly does manifesting work, you ask? Think about your heart's deepest desire or something that you want in life. It can be small or big. I will use the example from above to illustrate this technique. Think about how you would feel if you actually won the lottery. Speak it out loud and use the past tense as if you have already achieved it, "I won the lottery for $40 million!" Make sure you mean what you say every time you manifest something!

Think about how you are feeling after this claim of affirmation as if you have already won the lottery. I know you haven't won it yet but, for the sake of this exercise, how would you feel if you had? Ecstatic? Overjoyed? Like the king or queen of the world? Would you feel like you could do just about anything you wanted and be the happiest person on the entire planet now that you've won $40 million?

Now, let's put this into perspective. Think about how you are currently feeling with all of these emotions running through you right now. Is your heart getting excited? Do you notice a smile forming across your face? Perhaps this is a huge, ear-to-ear grin and not just a regular smile. When you are manifesting, wanting a desire to come true, think that it has already happened and you have already achieved it. Think past tense. You will feel all the butterflies in your tummy and also your insides warming up! These are normal feelings you feel when you accomplish something. Especially something that you may have originally thought would never happen or is a far-fetched notion. When something like that comes true, you'll be over the moon! Therefore, when you want something like that to come true, while you manifest, you must concentrate on feeling what you felt just moments ago. Feel that it has already happened for you. That thrill and exhilaration you feel when you say it out loud will make it happen for you soon enough! Of course, you also need to act on making it come true, so make sure you are buying those lottery tickets regularly. That was how many of the people in our meditation group won the second prize.

To take my skills to the next level, my Reiki Master asked both an older gentleman and me to sit down to see auras one quiet Saturday evening. This older gentleman was also in the Reiki Master level class with me. I did not know what my Reiki Master had meant by "auras" initially, but I was intrigued and wanted to learn. My Reiki Master then told us to concentrate on looking at his hands. He held his hands up in front of his chest and had his palms facing us while he rotated his wrists. Then he asked us to look at his third eye and soon enough, we both began to see colors around our Master's palms, hands, shoulders, head and neck. At that moment, a memory of when I was a child came flooding back, in which I remembered seeing colors around everything as a child. I never talked about this with anyone because I thought it was normal for everybody to see colors around everybody and everything. As I grew older, it got harder and harder to see colors. Eventually, I stopped seeing those colors and never even thought to question the loss of my ability. Now here I was, 19- to 20-years-old seeing colors around people and things again! This was *fantastic,* and it became a game for me! I challenged myself all the time. I would sit and watch people - stare at them even - to catch a glimpse of what their aura colors were. It was great, but most importantly, it was so much fun to see their colors from head to toe, around them and inside of them. It was pretty darn impressive! It worked on plants and animals too! It even worked on inanimate objects so if you would like to practice reading auras, stare at an object or look at your reflection in the mirror. It helps if you place yourself or the object against a white background.

Through Reiki, I also learned to read people, their energies and feel what they were feeling such as the kinds of issues they were suffering from, their emotions, pain, marital affairs, career, love, literally anything. I could even tell if they had an attachment with them that was draining their life force or energy. I did not know the terminologies until very recently but these are probably what people deemed psychic abilities and empathic abilities. Using my psychic and/or empathic abilities, I could easily read someone's past, present and future, see where their blockages were and see if their chakras were in alignment or whether they required work on specific ones. My ability to see people's auras also helped me to pinpoint the chakras and specific areas that required more attention during their sessions. This analysis helped with determining what we would target during a client's healing sessions that day.

Upon receiving my Reiki Master certification, I also started helping with the teaching aspect with my Reiki Masters at their

Reiki center. I thoroughly enjoyed imparting my knowledge to the students. It was fun to teach and just as fun to watch them absorb the material, and put their newly acquired knowledge and skills to the test. This was where I found my passion to teach people what I had learnt. Prior to that, teaching was a pain. Perhaps it depended on the material. The Reiki center eventually closed down but the teachings stayed with me. Most of the credit goes to my mother. If it were not for her, I would not have found my spiritual side. Therefore, I owe this to her for making sure that I went for Reiki and meditation sessions because it was so much more fun to do this together with my family in a place that felt like home. For having given me the chance to discover and develop my gifts, I want to thank both of my original Reiki Masters from the bottom of my heart for their teachings and guidance with every step during my five years there. They helped me discover myself in a way I otherwise would never have.

Life Beyond Reiki

At the Reiki center, not only did I learn meditation techniques, which incorporated manifestations, I even learned how to be a more patient person, a life skill which I greatly lacked. This new discovery of being able to ask the universe for whatever I wanted only made me manifest for so many more things, things that ended up coming true, like that four-digit story I shared earlier. I also got what I thought was my dream job of becoming a flight attendant through this process. Waiting for all of my manifestations to come true was truly testing my patience. As much as I started feeling dejected and got impatient when my wishes did not get fulfilled right away, when something was achieved, it felt incredible! On a side note, for those of you who are thinking about becoming flight attendants, try it! It was fun while it lasted but man, motion-sickness sucked! When I began understanding the power of manifestation, it became quite a shocking revelation for me, in a good way.

Apart from my ability to communicate with the divinities, I finally understood that I could also talk to spirits or ghosts. Some of you may have already figured that out from Chapter 1, however, this was something I was unaware of and obviously, I did not put two and two together until this point in time. As much as I did not enjoy communicating with the deceased, sometimes, all they wanted from me was help with going to the light. As I continued volunteering at the Reiki center, I encountered more and more of these beings and learnt to help them cross over into the light. Sometimes, when you are in a place and feel uneasy, it could be due to dark energies and entities. I learnt to clear the space of these beings as well. This was another skill my family and I heavily relied on as it became something we got accustomed to doing on a very regular basis and still do today from different parts of the world. One thing I grasped very quickly was that if there were beings that wanted to go to the light, there were also beings that didn't want to go there. If a spirit or being needed help, I would happily send them off to the light. I always made it a point to mention that I would never force anyone to go to the light if they did not want to because some of them were happy right where they were and were not bothering me. Then there were some beings that did not even come from the light but that's something we will not discuss right now.

Even though the Reiki center closed down in the end, my Master still looked out for his students. He came across this place that taught healing techniques and meditation with the ancient Egyptian divinities. I feel that somehow, everyone from all walks of life has an affiliation to Egypt for some rhyme or reason. At least, everyone that I have met has said that they loved Egypt even though they had never been there. This undying love probably has to do with how movies and documentaries portrayed the holy land. The mysteries; secrets of the unknown; the pyramids and other monuments there; potential secret passageways and hidden treasures in tombs; booby traps; mummies; the people; the history of the country; or a combination of some or all of the above notions just to name a few. I mean, there is no way I could disagree with anyone who tells me they loved Egypt. I felt the same way, and I had never been there!

Way before we even ventured into light work or spirituality, my mother and I were always attracted to oracle cards. She accumulated a massive collection and still has them in her house. She definitely has a lot of different oracle card decks, but which ones she actually uses is beyond my knowledge. I will tell you that she has more than enough and could honestly have her own store. Some of them are most probably still in their original packaging! Due to not knowing how to divine (read or interpret) the oracle cards, I stopped using most of the decks because I would ask a question, pull a card, then read the guidebooks to get my answers. Some of the statements from the guidebooks made sense but they were not entirely accurate for the specific questions I had asked. Or maybe they were accurate, and I just had difficulty understanding the messages, I don't know. I was also unable to pinpoint which message was specifically meant for me too. It was a relief to know that there were divination courses I could take that would help with this later on in my life.

Eventually, I enrolled in a few courses at this new Egyptian healing center. One of the courses I signed up for was, you guessed it, a divination course in which I learnt the art of divining oracle cards. Having already known how to communicate with the other divinities naturally, it was easy for me to connect with the ancient Egyptian divinities as well. Being able to tap into these ancient powers was a beautiful feeling. There was so much undiscovered potential in me that was ready to burst out and this was so exciting! I purchased my first ever ancient Egyptian divinities deck for the divination course to interpret the cards and must admit that the knowledge I gained helped me tremendously. I could not only talk to these powerful gods and goddesses, but could also channel them, as well as invite them into my body to speak directly through me. It was phenomenal to know that I could channel the divinities and also get accurate enough answers without really looking at the guidebook. It was all about connection and knowing who each god or goddess was and what he or she represented. Even after taking the course, I referred to the guidebook frequently. It started becoming easier to decipher the messages meant for me. Of course, when I channeled and the messages from the divinities got clearer with more practice, my reliance on the guidebook started decreasing.

There was never a name attached to the method in which I communicated with any of the divinities or deities growing up because I did not know what to call it. Was I channeling them my whole life without realizing it then? Either way, these were things that I have only ever seen in movies and read about in books. It felt as though a whole new world had opened up for me and swallowed me into this eternal abyss. It was mind-blowing! I loved this new feeling and at this point, I was merely getting my feet wet. Divination and channeling went hand-in-hand for me and at this time, it wasn't something I realized, but these were skills I would heavily rely upon later on in my life.

Discovering Astral Travel

Many of us have attempted meditation using various methods, some of us more successful than others. We have either acquired meditative techniques from our gurus or from videos we have watched. At this Egyptian healing center, I discovered something cool called astral traveling, which happens to be another form of meditation. What is that exactly and how does it work? Well, it is a technique used to help one travel during their meditative journeys. Think of Prue Halliwell from the first three seasons of Charmed (the original 1998 - 2006 series), where she would be sitting in one place but her soul would be astral projecting and it could be in another. Only, instead of trying to trick demons into thinking my astral self was the real me, I used this technique to travel back to the past – be it my current life's immediate past or any of my past lives – plus I could also travel to the future to see how things could turn out. No demon fighting for me. I battle with other things frequently enough and believe to already be living the Charmed life. Even for the experienced meditators, this was an entirely different ballgame. It was literally an out-of-body experience because when astral traveling, I was able to feel myself leaving my body and coming back into it every time. When this happens, it becomes harder for my physical body to breathe. My body does what it needs to do to stay alive for as long as I am astral traveling in this meditative state. It is difficult for me to take my usual deep breaths. My breathing is short, shallow and makes me feel like I am asphyxiating. Okay, I just realized that the way I described this process sounds terrifying as hell, but it isn't as scary as I somehow seemed to have made it out to be. When my journey was complete and I was fully back inside of my body after accomplishing my task, I reverted to breathing normally again. The transition is very smooth. During my initial stages of practicing astral traveling, I found it mind boggling to know that such a technique really existed and that it was within the grasp of my fingertips! I frequently astral travel now, to the Egyptian temples and other places of worship to meditate and bathe in the energies that are there!

During my time here at the Egyptian healing center, I also learnt how to use the healing powers of the ancient Egyptian divinities to heal others and myself. Not only did I tap into the universal Reiki energy, at times, I also harnessed the powers of these mighty gods and goddesses by invoking them to help with healing sessions. While I never practiced healing anyone at the Egyptian healing center, I took various courses with my mother and sister to learn numerous skill sets to enhance my gifts and abilities. Most of the time when I was at home, I practiced a lot on myself and felt my powers and abilities growing significantly because of the beings I worked with. The teacher I had was planning a trip to

Egypt, but since the unrest was going on at the time, this never came to fruition.

I had spent a total of seven years walking the spiritual path by this time. Unfortunately, my journey with this place lasted barely a year as I left Singapore, my home, in January 2014 and immigrated to the U.S. to pursue my bachelor's degree. My family, of course, stayed behind. They continued growing in their spiritual journey while mine sadly took a turn for the worse. Without my family and community to practice with, I barely had the motivation to meditate, let alone do anything else. I went on a long, tumultuous, almost seven-year hiatus from my spiritual life.

The Seven-Year Glitch

During my seven-year break from spirituality, my entire being was back to how it was before my first ever Reiki session at 18. This meant that I was getting angry at the drop of a hat again and my impatience returned probably tenfold. I went back to hating everyone and was rude to most people. I simply despised the human race, period and thus returning to not being a people person.

All this could have had something to do with me missing my family and friends back at home too, or it could have just been me being me because that was how I was for most of my life until Reiki came into my life. It wasn't just a phase. That was how I was as a person! I was terrified that I had completely lost touch with my spiritual side, and then, the trip of a lifetime chanced upon me! A trip to Egypt in November and December of 2019! This trip was not with the teacher who originally taught me to tap into the powers of the ancient Egyptian divinities, but another teacher that my mother had found. Both of these teachers studied the same techniques from another teacher, so it was great that the new teacher was organizing this trip! It was her first time organizing such a trip on her own and she had many students, including my mother, who wanted to go. I might not have been her student, but because I took some courses prior, I was able to join them on this adventure of a lifetime! I truly was grateful for this opportunity! The best parts of this trip were reconnecting with my mother in person after three whole years and getting to spend three weeks together in this holy land!

Having been stagnant in my spiritual journey meant that I wasn't the nicest person to be around, even on this trip of a lifetime. During the trip, I complained a lot and yelled at people. Not at the people in my group, but I got annoyed at others and yelled at them. Remember when I said I got angry at the drop of a hat? Apparently, it made no difference what continent I was on. As soon as the anger hit, I exploded. Picture a volcano erupting. Yeah, that was how I was when I vented! Despite that, the trip to Egypt was absolutely life-changing! I got back into meditation while I was there and was once again able to feel energies around me. It was all thanks to the mystical, spiritual aspects of Egypt herself but it also had to do with the group I traveled with. We were all there for the same reasons: to learn, to get in touch with our spiritual side, to pay homage to the great ancient ones who gave us so much, and to relish in all things Egypt. In addition to getting back in touch with my spiritual side rather quickly, I was also able to invoke the divinities into my physical body and channel them! That was a major feat for me! I did that once or twice in what seemed like eons ago, but being able to tap back into all of it was very encouraging and motivating for me. Perhaps this would be my spiritual comeback!

Lacking the practice of my spirituality throughout the last six years meant that my temper was very apparent to just about anyone. It was a little difficult to keep it under control. Since reconnecting and getting back in touch with my spiritual side seemed very quick and seamless, I didn't want to let this opportunity go. I came back home to the U.S. with so much energy and started meditating again, hoping to keep my temper in check and continuing to enhance my spiritual growth. Having all that energy inspired and motivated me, and so I started getting back into my spiritual groove. Wanting to maintain all that I had gained while I was in the holy land of Egypt made me feel more confident and excited than ever. Guess what? That didn't last long at all. Within a few weeks of my return, I got sick and tired of being forlorn in my journey again. It was frustrating to not get anywhere with all of the meditating that I had been doing. At the same time, I also didn't know what needed to be done since there was no community for me to rely on for support, motivation, encouragement or guidance of any sort. I started dwindling yet again.

Alas, the Corona virus pandemic hit.

Finding My Way Home to Reiki

All this time, I was pursuing my MBA, which has been stressful. On top of that, I was having problems with two things in particular. The first had to do with an issue in my personal life; the second was a problem with my house itself, which I will discuss in Chapter 9. The first problem led me to constantly chide my husband and cause him even more stress in addition to whatever he was already going through. Knowing that something needed to be done, self-realization hit me: Why am I being such a bitch to everyone? Why am I getting annoyed at every little thing? Why am I taking it out on the entire world? I know what you're thinking and no, I did not cause or manifest the pandemic! I haven't even been meditating properly let alone manifesting anything. *Hello!?*

However, still being spiritual in some ways, I knew the universe works wonders and gives you everything you want, or in my case, need, when it's your time to have it. All you need to do is put it out there and the universe will take care of it. Although I was not looking for any signs, in June or July of 2020, because of the problems I mentioned above, I decided that it was time for me to change. I knew I needed to change my behavior towards others, keep my temper in check and not lose my patience with everything and everyone. As soon as my thoughts materialized, advertisements of Reiki classes started popping up on Facebook. I hadn't even thought about or talked about Reiki in ages and there it was, staring me in the face from this social media app. Reiki, the impetus for my breakthrough to becoming a slightly better person; the epitome of my spirituality. I took it as a sign from the universe that it was reaching out to me to tell me, "Hey kiddo, we've got your back, and it's about time you got back in the spiritual saddle," and without hesitation, I clicked on the advertisement. The course was even on sale, so I purchased this online Reiki course. Who knew online spiritual courses existed? I was one lucky girl!

Back to the basics! After making the purchase, I attacked the course like never before. I was determined to complete this within the week. Thinking that as a once certified Reiki Master myself, it would be easy to understand the materials and I would be able to complete the course by the end of the week. Little did I know there were so many various types of Reiki and what I was learning through this online course was no doubt similar to what I had learnt back in Singapore, but also so distinctive. I also noticed that there were so many differences from what I had originally learnt and taught others.

You may wonder why I decided to spend money learning something that I had already learned, completed and mastered once before. Heck, I was even teaching this to others! Of course, I remembered everything! I think. Reiki was a part of me! I was fully aware that I could just put my hands on my body to heal myself. The thing is, I couldn't feel the heat in my hands and I had doubts about whether or not I was healing. I knew I should not have doubts about this, but there they were. Therefore, one of the reasons for pursuing this was to get reattuned to the Reiki energy through the attunements I would be receiving. Another crucial benefit I foresaw was relearning anything that I could have forgotten from before. Taking a Reiki course with someone different was great because I ended up learning so much more! Today, I feel as though I could have missed out on a lot if the universe didn't guide me to study Reiki with another Master. I mean, I knew of distance healing but this online course taught us to attune people from a distance too! Was this always possible? To be able to attune a person from afar was not something I was taught at 18!

This Master who taught me Reiki online had a Facebook group. "Yes! I finally found my community!" I thought to myself. This was a place where I felt safe and comfortable in because there were like-minded people just like me, all over the entire world! How cool was that! How did I not know about this? Slowly, I started taking more online spiritual courses from various teachers and practiced what I had learned with members of all the different Facebook communities I was joining.

By October of 2020, I was part of at least five different Facebook groups that all had the theme of spirituality in common. We were all learning, growing and developing our skills. Some groups allowed you to practice with other members while others did not. Either way, all these groups let you share your experiences, ask questions and participate in discussions. Through these methods, I thought I was also learning, growing and developing my skills just like the others. We were all on different levels. Although I had my Reiki experiences and abilities before I left Singapore, I felt very new and inexperienced because of the intermission I took from my spiritual journey. It seemed as though I was restarting my entire spiritual voyage, and honestly, in a way, I was.

Sad to say that I still wasn't meditating regularly, but I was more involved in the groups because I found my people, right? Sure. The thing is, I knew that I was still slowly adjusting to getting back my abilities and gifts. What I did not understand was why on earth it was taking me so long to be at the level I used to be at in 2012 and 2013 when I was at my peak. I was losing my mind and my patience - which was first and foremost never my best virtue as you know by now - and somehow, I couldn't understand why this was happening to me or more so why it was *not* happening for me. I was having a tough time connecting with the ancient Egyptian divinities and all the other divinities that I used to have regular conversations with, even Jesus, Mother Mary, Ganesha and the other Hindu gods and goddesses. It was devastating! I now had two stacks of oracle cards of the ancient Egyptian divinities that I didn't know how to use because I had forgotten what I had learnt from my divination course. Even when I was in Egypt, I was unable to refresh my memory. Some of the names of the divinities came back to me but who each god or goddess was, what they represented, I couldn't for the life of me figure out without looking in the guidebook or doing some research online.

Maybe I was being too hard on myself because we all needed to start somewhere and that was exactly what the guidebooks were there for. I know! My rational mind knows this now but back then, during a time when my desperation to progress was eminent, I found all of this extremely frustrating. After taking all of these courses, my inability to practice to the fullest extent was due to my lack of meditation? "That's ridiculous," I thought, but it really wasn't. The thing is, I could not sit still and meditate. I was unable to focus. One thing or another always ended up constantly distracting me. Sometimes it was my dog. At other times, it was my husband, my brother-in-law or all three of them. Then sometimes, the distraction was caused by something else entirely.

My house echoes, so no matter which part of the house I was in, I could hear at least one of them, if not all of them. Neither did I have a quiet place to do this nor the time. On top of working full-time, there was school homework that needed to be completed. Then when my husband and I were home, we would have dinner and watch television together. Sometimes, all I wanted to do was watch television on my own and catch up on my programs when I had completed my homework. I neither had the time nor the patience to sit down and meditate. Was it honestly the lack of meditation that was holding me back from soaring?

Humbug! All those things were excuses that I told myself just to avoid meditating. Does this sound familiar to you? If you are like me, you would have found all sorts of excuses to get out of your personal development too. Or maybe you came up with excuses to get out of doing your chores, even if it was something as simple as washing your plate after you have eaten. Ever since I can remember, I came up with all kinds of excuses to get out of doing my homework. Being the queen of excuses, there was nothing short of a creative excuse that I could come up with to do my homework. Of course, I did everything else that I wanted to do except for the constant procrastination for what I really needed to be doing. Then again, I enjoyed my spirituality! I loved it! It never felt like a chore. I hated homework and still hate homework, considering I am currently pursuing a master's program. Then what in the world was the reason for my not wanting to meditate?

Then it hit me so hard in my third eye and my crown chakra. I realized I conjured up all of these excuses not because I didn't *want* to meditate, but more so because I felt as though my growth was stunted. I felt that I was not progressing, or at least not progressing the way I wanted to, rapidly, and that wasn't happening. I wanted to be at my peak like I was in 2012 and 2013 and it didn't even feel close to how I felt after my first Reiki session. That was why I had all these sorry reasons for excuses. Not my husband, not the dog, not work, not school, not the lack of a quiet place, just the lack of progression in my spiritual growth and that was what was keeping me from doing what I needed. Feeling unmotivated because I was not accomplishing anything made me come to a complete standstill, plain and simple.

What I had failed to realize back then through all of this was that fortunately, there definitely was some type of progress. It was minuscule and excruciatingly slow, but it was there. Obviously, I know this now because if my progress were still stagnant, I would not be at the spiritual level I am today.

By now, I was slowly running out of excuses because school wouldn't begin again until January 2021, which meant that I could work on some other online spiritual courses in the meantime. And so that was what I did. One course in particular that intrigued me had to do with reading the Akashic Records, which was what one would call the book of the soul. I signed up for two online courses with different instructors because I wanted to learn various ways to access the records and see what worked best for me. Just like how studying Reiki with two separate masters taught me different techniques, provided me with multiple insights and perspectives, I figured with the Akashic Records, there would be differences too. True enough, as with anything else, both teachings were vastly different.

As the months went by, it was now January 2021 and school recommenced, so my spiritual studies went on a mini-break. I might not have been meditating full-time, but I was trying to get a little bit in here and there, as and when I could, in between classes, work, and family life. I made sure to heal myself using Reiki as often as possible, so that was helping to keep me somewhat calm and patient. Thankfully, my husband is a very supportive and understanding man. We still spent a lot of time together as any couple should, but he also understood when I asked for some personal space. It worked out because he did his own thing when I did mine, so there was a good balance between us.

Double, Double, Toil & Trouble – I Was In Trouble

My spirituality came back to me at a very crucial point in my life, sometime in March of 2020 when the pandemic hit and we were all forced to stay at home in the most unexpected of ways. The universe always gives you signs to preempt you to prepare yourself for a challenge that was soon coming your way. I received those signs all the time. Did I listen right away? No! Absolutely not! During this time, I was having different issues in the house. This particular issue pertains to the second issue I had mentioned in the first paragraph of Chapter 8.

Previously, I had briefly talked about beings that did not even come from the light. I will address those beings in this chapter, not in detail, but enough for you to know what I meant by the phrase "beings that did not even come from the light." You all have heard the sayings about monsters hiding in the closet or under the bed, haven't you? If you have, then perhaps you can relate. These monsters or beings were always hiding in my bedroom closet. Initially, this was manageable. Beings would come looking for me from everywhere, not just my closet, to ask for help to be sent to the light and when they came my way, I helped them with this. However, when it started getting overwhelming and almost unbearable, I knew something was wrong and that I had to increase my powers. My abilities at this point were weak and very mild so the universe was giving me signs to wake up and smell the bloody coffee. And I hate coffee!

When there are beings that need to go into the light, I get a very specific sign. It is a very specific type of headache. That was their way of informing me of their presence. Yet, despite heeding those signs and sending them to the light, if the headache persisted and failed to disappear after some time, I knew for a fact that something was amiss. It wasn't just the residue from the beings that had already been sent to the light earlier; it was so much more than that. As I was still weaker and in the process of slowly growing and rebuilding my powers, I reached out to my mother and sister, who were still practicing their gifts that had escalated to a whole other level. The two of them had grown so significantly over the last seven-plus years, whereas I had not, so I felt it was best to seek their expertise to check on why these beings kept coming even though I had been continuously sending them to the light. They kept coming one after another, sometimes individually and at other times in groups. It was impossible to even take a breather or do my work because I was overwhelmed by their unwanted presence. Clearly they were coming inside my house too, but at this time, I did not know that my master bedroom walk-in closet was the main entrance and exit point. Maybe you already guessed it, but don't jump the gun! I will get to why I said that soon enough.

I mentioned the universe always gives you signs. I ignored the initial signs and these beings started coming more and more frequently, as if my house was theirs. When they came, I would do my thing and send them to the light. But then they started attacking my home and my dog. My house was supposed to be an impenetrable fortress, but due to my disconnect from all-things spiritual, these beings were able to enter my house. I continued with my usual process of constantly sending them to the light, and it would stop for a little bit. At first, I never thought much about it, but the universe and divinities were desperately urging me to build up my abilities and gifts again. Why I never listened to their first twenty-million different warning signs ever, I don't know and will never understand. They always gave me a heads up about something that I would need to brace myself for and I would completely brush it aside thinking it wasn't going to be anything major. Yeah, it usually wasn't, until it was! I wish I had listened to their first warning sign because I was about to face something very terrible. This would be nothing like your everyday passer-by spirits that needed help going to the light.

My husband can't feel anything so he was not affected by these entities and non-light beings. Yup, I said it. These weren't your "Casper-the-friendly-ghost" types. They were otherworldly monsters inside my closet. True, my husband felt nothing but I wish I could say the same about our dog. This poor girl was a happy-go-lucky six-year-old dog when I had first met her and my husband in 2016. She had no paranormal encounters until I married into the family. Although I wasn't actively pursuing my spirituality, when I first discovered the issues in our house in 2019, I could still feel everything because I had my spiritual powers within me and I could tap into them whenever I wanted to. Actually, it was more like my powers and abilities would fulminate off me and take over to warn me and help me. The attacks were manageable in 2019 and were rather rare, maybe once every few months. As usual, the normal procedure and automatic reaction was to send them to the light. It was easy.

When the stay-at-home policy was put in place in March of 2020, the frequency of the attacks increased tremendously and was on an almost daily basis now. Unfortunately, my powers were very mild due to the lack of practice and I knew I had to build them back up. I needed to be strong to combat whatever these uninvited beings were and whenever they made unwanted guest appearances in my house, unannounced.

These issues weren't just affecting me; it was taking a physical, emotional, and mental toll on my now 10-year-old dog who trembled vigorously from fear every time she felt these entities and non-light beings. Considering she had never been exposed to anything like this before she met me, it became such a horrific experience for her! It was devastating to watch her go through what she did, that poor dog! It happened daily now! She was so frightened that she tried to scratch her way through the walls to escape! If I were lying down in bed, she would climb on top of my head and try to find a way to get higher up. If she were a cat, she'd be clinging for dear life from the ceiling! That was how petrified she was! There were times my dog refused to enter my master bedroom. She would stand right outside the door looking at me and then she would go to the other end of the house. Even when I called her to come to me, she would come, but she stood right outside the doorway, refusing to step foot into the master bedroom. Soon, even I knew something wasn't right about the master bedroom because of those specific headaches I would get just by being in there. Compared to other parts of the house where I felt uneasy, the headaches intensified in the master bedroom, specifically in the walk-in closet. It's strange but when I was in bed, my dog sometimes went into the closet, scratched the wall frantically, then would run out of the bedroom entirely and never come back inside for some time. Maybe she was trying to warn me about the closet after all but I just never understood?

These encounters we had carried on for months at a time and I had a feeling – get ready for this – that my house was a portal to the lower dimensions. Perhaps some of you believers already had your speculations about this from a few paragraphs before. The rest of you might be wondering what made me come to such a conclusion? Well, here's a story for you. My old bedroom in my mother's house in Singapore was like that too. We had uninvited visitors coming and going at all hours of the day. My closed laptop without a battery, which was not plugged into the wall outlet to charge, would turn on and light up at 3 a.m. almost daily. Freaky? YES! It scared the shit out of me! My mother's house had portals which explained the freakiness that went on at all hours of the day and night. As I had experiences with portals before, I wanted a second opinion about my own house. Look, I might not have been as powerful or as spiritual as I once was during 2020, but my gifts and abilities were still within me, trying to break free and I knew that I needed help with this. It was not something I could handle alone. Hence, I asked my sister, who, to my dismay, confirmed that my house wasn't just a portal, but it contained multiple portals, and it was *the vessel* that allowed for non-light beings and/or dark entities to enter and exit as they pleased. The central portal was the master bedroom closet. That explained a lot. I mean, how messed up was that?

I knew I needed to do something to keep the portals closed. Otherwise, the dog and I would have gone ballistic. We were already really affected by this so I consulted my sister on what I had to do. She was able to connect with the divinities easily and asked me to perform specific rituals she downloaded with the guidance of the gods and goddesses to help me keep the portals sealed, but these rituals were something I had to repeat monthly. It was tedious, but I had to keep my home and my family safe, so I made this ritual a routine to be completed within the first three days of every month to ensure the portals remained sealed. Otherwise, it would be too late and we would have had the unwanted visitors again. It would work for a while, but then I was one person. My family was not physically with me to help close the portals shut permanently. The seals I placed on the portals would slowly start to crack open, allowing some beings to slip through the cracks into my house. Some of them came in incognito and it would take me days to realize I had "guests." Then there were others that would let me know of their presence right away. Some were happy to go to the light, others couldn't and the rest didn't want to. The things that came out from the portals were getting stronger and I quickly recognized that if I didn't build my powers up, I would not be able to fight or protect my family and my property. I refused to allow these things to take over my life. This was my life and my house, and I was in control!

Double, Double, Toil & Trouble – Reclaiming What's Mine

Thankfully, come June 2021 (yes, it took a whole year because of school, work and other obligations), I was done with my MBA classes for a bit and went back to resume finishing my Akashic Records courses, both of them. It took some time but eventually, I completed both of the courses that contained different teaching methods. I managed to somehow fuse both of the teachings and reached out to people in the various Facebook groups I was in to let me practice doing Akashic Record readings for them. In my attempts to hone my spirituality, I started offering free readings and healing sessions and got a free flow of practice clients. The constant practice was crucial for my growth and I am grateful for all the people who gave me the opportunity to practice on them. Both of these courses required me to constantly meditate before tapping into my own records to do readings. During this time, my tenacity to persevere with my spiritual growth was profound. As it was already difficult for me to sustain my practice initially, ensuring I got enough daily practice to do readings and healing sessions for others was not only motivating, but also allowed me to spiritually grow much faster. It took a lot of practice, patience and perseverance to keep at it but I wanted it so badly, so I did the work. And I loved doing this. Doing readings for people was fun, heck, it is fun! When I did a healing session for someone and they told me afterwards that they felt great, that was the best feeling ever. Meditating daily became a priority for me and got me into the groove of nurturing my gifts and abilities as I knew it would come in handy at some point when I needed to fight the monsters in my closet. I was finally listening to the universe! This was a constant struggle because while I was fighting to toughen up, they were fighting to break open the seals. Hoping to get some support and answers, I reached out to one of the groups about the portals.

8. Page 40 needs a period at the end of "master's program":

".....again, I enjoyed my spirituality! I loved it! It never felt like a chore. I hated homework and still hate homework, considering I am currently pursuing a master's program.!

Surprisingly, no one would believe that negative entities were affecting me and my house. As if that wasn't enough to disappoint me, many of them said that there are no such things as negative entities. Some comments were blatantly nasty. The people in the group ended up blaming my fears and said that I was manifesting this. I was in disbelief! How could multiple people feel that there were no such things as beings that were *not of light*? Have you not watched The Exorcist, The Conjuring movies or any horror movies? I mean, I garnered so much flack and hostility from a group that I thought I belonged in. I felt so alone and finally realized that I was! It sucked to not be able to receive help from a spiritual group in what I thought contained like-minded people like me. It was messed up and devastating that they said such horrible things.

I felt dejected because even my support group didn't help or believe me. After all, they didn't believe in these things themselves. Who else could I turn to? After wallowing about and talking to my mother and sister, I figured all I could continue to do was the monthly rituals and at some point in my life, when my powers and abilities grew, I would get a download of some sort from the divinities that would assist me with my woes. Or, perhaps the world would open up again and my family could fly here and come help permanently shut these things down. Unfortunately, my family did not know how to shut down portals. As for the portal that was in my mother's house, someone helped with that about a decade ago and closed it permanently, but I didn't even think to reach out to them when I needed to get this situation sorted out.

The post was in vain. No one cared to help me because the people in that group who commented were a bunch of non-believers when it came to the negative energies. Subsequently, after my post about these portals, a lady created a post about wanting to practice reading the Akashic Records with someone as she had just completed the course herself. I commented and said I would love to be her practice partner as I had also just completed the course myself and could use the practice. Upon completing the readings for each other, she mentioned that she saw my post from earlier and could assist me with the portals. I didn't tell her how many there were or give her a backstory about it, but she mentioned there were multiple portals in various parts of the house. I was both shocked and amazed at the same time that someone finally believed me and was willing to help me! She knew! She was able to detect where they all were! She walked me through what I needed to do and that was that! My house is no longer a vessel now! I still have the verbiage should the need ever arise that I or someone else would require it.

It was the best thing I could have asked for at the time. When I said earlier that the universe gives you what you want when you ask for it, it really does! This lady helped me with something I would never have been able to otherwise figure out on my own and for that, I am truly grateful to her and the universe for bringing us together. With her, I was able to also practice more Akashic Record readings, something I had come to enjoy doing tremendously. She also gave me the confidence about charging people for the readings I did because according to her, I was remarkably accurate. She gave me the confidence booster that was much needed for me to continue with growing as a reader and a healer as well. It was refreshing to hear from an experienced person that I was good at what I did, especially since I was starting afresh after an almost eight-year hiatus now.

Enhancing My Abilities – The Akashic Records & Channeling

While I was working on completing both of the Akashic Records courses, I meditated and practiced reading my own Akashic records daily too. On top of meditation, I also started doing one-card pulls every day using my ancient Egyptian divinities oracle decks for myself. I had two decks and worked with both of them. This was a whole routine for me. I would start with my grounding techniques or protection. Afterward, I would meditate, manifest, do my card pulls, practice my Akashic Record readings for myself, and then do a karmic release, not necessarily in that order, but that was the routine. I spent about three hours total daily, working on myself and growing my abilities. I restarted this journey sometime in June of 2021 after completing my MBA classes for the year and continue to practice mindfulness and meditation to this day. Having closed the portals and shut down the vessel, it was apparent that I had to continue getting stronger. It wasn't just to protect my loved ones and my home anymore; it was also to get back to being able to do what I loved doing. I thoroughly enjoyed doing readings for people and healing them. It was such a beautiful gift, and I wanted to embrace it to the fullest extent.

I have been talking a lot about the Akashic Records and how much I love doing such readings. For those of you who have been wondering what the Akashic Records are, allow me to provide you with some insight. Earlier in Chapter 8, I mentioned that the Akashic Records are the books of the soul. Where are these books kept and whose soul am I talking about? Imagine a library full of books that contained every single thing that has ever happened in your life. Simply put, these books contain your life stories. Now imagine that your soul has lived multiple lifetimes in the past and it will continue to live even more lifetimes in the future. Including your present life, this library holds books of every single incident that has ever happened and incidents that will be happening in every single life that your soul has been in and will continue to be in existence for. Libraries do not contain just one type of book, so the Akashic Records library will not just have books of your soul. It would contain books of the souls of every single person and living thing that has ever existed, not just on this planet but on any plane, dimension or realm that these souls have ever lived on. Does that make sense? Think about all the people you know. They all have stories, so all of their books are contained in this library along with yours and everyone else's. These records or books (the terms are interchangeable so call them what you'd like to) are kept in a universal library for readers to access when they need to look into just about anything pertaining to the client's past, present or future. As a reader, I get to see what past issues have been brought forward into the present life that are still affecting the person I am reading for. These past issues can either be something from one's multiple past lives or even something from the immediate past of the present life. For example, a present life issue from the immediate past would be childhood traumas that this person is still suffering from today as an adult. Many of us have gone through hell as children. We may not realize it, but we are subconsciously still holding on to the pain and suffering as adults. The Akashic Records can reveal all of that.

I can access my own Akashic Records easily, but if I wanted to secretly do a reading for a famous celebrity for the fun of it, I would not be able to access their records. That is because all these records are protected by guardians and are very private. In order for me to access my favorite celebrity's records, for instance, I would require his or her permission to even be able to go near those records. The guardians will just not allow it.

Anyone who works closely with the Akashic Records can read those books and provide detailed answers to whatever questions are being asked, be it your own or someone else's. It is very easy for me to access my own records now. To access someone else's records, however, the reader requires the person's full legal name and his or her permission. For instance, let's say I wanted to access my sister's Akashic Records, I know her full legal name, obviously, but I would need her permission to get into her records to do a reading for her. Without her permission, the guardians will simply not allow me to access her records. Let's say she paid me to do a reading for her instead. By paying me this sum of money, my sister is directly telling me that she wants me to do a reading for her. The universe now sees this form of exchange, so when I access her records, permission is implied. As the reader, I also take it a step further and inform her guardians that I received payment to do this reading for her and that the payment is my sister's way of permitting me to obtain access to those records. This is my way of crossing the Ts and dotting the Is. The guardians will accept this and grant me full access to her records for the reading.

I will share a funny story with you, and then you will understand why I am so particular about the minute details mentioned above. When I was practicing Akashic Record readings with my family and friends, my mother had given me permission to do a reading for her. She had numerous questions and along with those questions she gave me her permission through a text message to do her reading. I opened her records, received the answers to all the questions and closed her records, thanking all the divinities and the universe for allowing me to do this reading for her. After giving her the reading, my mother asked me another question to which she needed answers. I figured I could easily go back into her records and retrieve the information she needed because I had literally just closed out of her records from the first reading. Nope. That was a no-go. I asked the question for her and her guardian who kept her records told me very firmly, "No."

Hmm. Okay. Let's try again! I explained that I just completed doing a reading for her a while ago and she had another question she had asked me, and that was my reason for coming back. All I heard was dead silence. There was no answer. Did they already forget that I was in there just a couple of minutes earlier? Getting a little tired of this game, I asked why I wasn't able to get the answers to the question she was asking now when they gave me everything willingly before. It was my mother! Guess what the guardian said? "Because it is none of your business! It is not your place to know!"

It was said in a very matter-of-fact manner. I was so taken aback by that fierce tone. Clearly, these guardians took their jobs very seriously and will not let anyone slip through the cracks to gain access to books they shouldn't have access to. It made sense, but this was perplexing. I literally had access just moments ago! How was I going to get the answer for my mother then? I went back to my phone and scrolled through the chain of messages between my mother and myself and realized that she did not grant me permission to access her records for that single question she had asked. She insisted she did and I had to remind her that she did indeed give me permission for the first reading, and I had opened and closed the books. Since she asked the final question *after* I had closed her books, she needed to give me her permission again for the second reading. Remember, if you ever need to go back and reopen someone's records after you have closed them, make sure to get their permission again! Especially if it is a free reading that you are doing for them. After she gave me her permission for the second time, the guardians had no trouble letting me access her records. Crazy isn't it? It was great to know that no one will be able to access anyone's records without the owner's permission, but then to actually have experienced their wrath (I feel them staring daggers at me for using this word, but the word feels apt in this situation) was quite a different feeling altogether.

When I was working on both the courses, I was required to meditate a lot so that I was in the proper state of mind before accessing my records. If you're asking whether or not I worked on both of the courses simultaneously, no, I did not. I completed one before starting the other. It would have been way too complicated to do them both concurrently because the teachings and methods of accessing the records were vastly different. The two Akashic Records courses were both very helpful to my spiritual growth. As much as I incorporated both the teachings into one, I ended up finding my own groove – with the guidance of the gods and goddesses – to access not just mine but anyone's records (with their permission). Both of the courses gave me long-winded methods to access these records, but with the guidance of the divinities, it wasn't as lengthy anymore. Furthermore, I was still able to get all of the information that I needed once I had accessed the records. One teacher's method was to read from literal books that the Akashic Records library contained and the other teacher's method was to listen to what was being said instead. I found it difficult to physically open up a book and read the words in them. Since I was a channeler by nature, it was much easier for me to obtain the information using the latter more so than the former. I tried both ways and stuck with the one I gelled with more.

With my powers, abilities and gifts growing day by day, I also started becoming very active in my groups, even the group that belittled my questions and concerns about the portals. Additionally, I joined more groups that allowed me to practice and enhance my abilities freely. I would offer free readings to people in various groups. Initially, I received a mixture of both positive and negative reviews, especially for plain psychic readings in which I would either tap into a person's energy and read them or read them by looking at their pictures. Some people called this cold psychic or intuitive readings as well. There were hits and misses. I was very confident in my Akashic Record readings but not so much when it came to my psychic readings. Let me admit that it was weird because I relied on psychic readings when I volunteered at the Reiki center in Singapore but it was so hard to do a simple reading for someone using that skill now. As I became much more confident with the ancient

Egyptian divinities oracle cards, I started doing one-card readings for people in those very groups.

My initial hesitation was not knowing every single divinity in the deck. I did not know who they were, what they did or what they would or could potentially say. Working with those cards daily since June 2021 as part of my three-hour meditation routine enabled me to build a much stronger bond with the cards and the divinities.

Remember I complained about how I was having a difficult time deciphering the cards and their messages and had to constantly use the guidebook to look up what the cards meant? Well, my rational brain kicked in and told me that the guidebook was there to guide me so that I could familiarize myself with the divinities and the definitions. The ancient Egyptian divinities reaffirmed that too, luckily. I listened this time, stopped complaining, and started doing one-card pulls for myself. I used the guidebook to constantly guide me when doing my readings until I was asked to do a reading for myself without looking at the book at all. I was very hesitant and voiced my concern to the divinities about not being ready. The gods and goddesses were always very patient with me and constantly encouraged me. If the card I pulled that day was one they knew I had already pulled many times before, they would say to me, "Don't look at the book. You've gotten this one before. You know what it is about, now you channel me (whichever god or goddess was on the card)."

After channeling their message for the day for myself or receiving answers to my various questions, I was allowed to look in the guidebook for further guidance and explanations. That was how I learnt. It was insane. I was so afraid that I was listening to my very own thoughts half the time because how can they know what I am going through or what I am thinking of, right? Wrong! They know everything. They're the gods and goddesses!

With lots of practice, I began to tell the difference between my mind's voice and that of the divinities'. The ability to differentiate between the two would become my lifeline and the core of my very being when I did readings for others later down the road.

My Spiritual Growth Spurt

When I was finally able to distinguish between the two - my mind voice and my intuition or the voices of the divinities - for my readings, I started reading for other people, especially using my oracle cards and reading the Akashic Records. My hesitation when it came to plain psychic readings persisted because it was still more difficult for me. A friend and mentor of mine did a reading for me about this and said I was using the Akashic Records reading as a crutch when I read for others. Can you believe that? Funnily enough, I knew she was right because I was a channeler; I could hear the messages intuitively and pass them on to people just by reading or tapping into their energies. Wasn't this how I was able to read people back in Singapore when all I did was study and practice Reiki? I had no need to access anything else or use other modalities to read someone.

The original guinea pigs who volunteered to let me practice were my mother and sister. Of course, who else would it be? Then some friends and extended family asked for readings too. Again, I was very skeptical because I knew all of these people so well. What if it was my mind telling me things that I already knew about them when I did readings for them? Naturally, I had self-doubts and whenever I did, I got scolded. The way the divinities scolded me was rather hilarious, by the way, so it always cracked me up. It was never demeaning or derogatory. They talked to me the way they would a friend because we have that type of relationship now. The self-doubts came about because, at times, when I did a reading, it would sound like the message was meant for me. That was when I would get skeptical and think or ask them, "Are you sure this is for them and not for me?" The divinities always responded with a simple "yes" to that question every time.

The more readings I did for my loved ones, the more I realized that I was not clouded by my own, personal knowledge of them. Every reading that I did was 100 percent guided by the divinities. I know this because I always asked for feedback for every reading I gave, even when I started reading for paying clients. Whether it was a good reading or one I completely botched, be it a paid or an unpaid reading, because when the feedback came, I would understand that those messages were indeed meant for the recipient I was reading for and not for me. I received a lot of positive reviews from these clients and all these positive reviews only further boosted my confidence level. In turn, I finally accepted that my readings were truly guided by the divinities and that it was not at all my mind telling me what my clients needed to hear. YES!

As soon as my confidence level increased, my natural abilities started to shine. My psychic readings still needed work, but divining these two ancient Egyptian divinities oracle card decks have been something that kept getting easier and easier for me to do. I loved how I connected with these gods and goddesses and how I could even joke with some of them and have regular conversations with them. Archangel Michael is very easy for most people to connect with. He is a very vain Archangel who can be such a comedian and makes me laugh until my stomach and cheekbones hurt. He might not be from either one of my decks and he certainly isn't an ancient Egyptian divinity, but he is one of my go-to divinities for literally anything, especially when I could use a good laugh, major protection and grounding, and clearing of space.

It is bizarre to think that we mere mortals can have marvelous relationships with such powerful divinities. Perhaps, it isn't that crazy after all, considering I had full-fledged conversations with the Hindu gods and goddesses, Jesus and Mother Mary, practically my entire life! I am sure if I experienced this, other people would have too! Perhaps you did! I could never tell anyone this when I was a child as people would have deemed me insane and probably thrown me into a mental institution. It wasn't even something I thought I could tell my mother about, not that I even considered it to begin with. Think about it. If our family didn't even talk about something as simple as the ability to communicate with or hear ghosts, how could we possibly talk about communicating with the divinities? Gods and goddesses? Nope. This was most certainly kept under the radar for a long time. It seemed like a forbidden topic until we started experiencing more paranormal activities when we began our spiritual journey in Reiki. After that, during meditations, we would get messages from the divinities. It was during this time that we slowly began addressing the topics that were once so taboo to speak of in our house when I was growing up.

All About Meditation

I remember my very first meditation. The initial stages were tough because my mind wasn't blank and I did not know how to keep it from wandering. I was young and had no experience in this field whatsoever. I could not sit still and fidgeted a lot. I constantly thought about food, danced in my head, sang songs in my mind and even literally bobbed to the tunes - I had choreographed an entire dance routine to full songs sometimes as well – and I spoke to random people that would come across my mind. Some of these people who popped into my meditations were people I had never even met before! I was never taught to acknowledge any of these thoughts and let them go before resuming my meditation, but I knew I had to silence my mind and so, I would, only to have everything that I had asked to go away before flow right through again. It was a vicious cycle: to think about something during a meditation session and tell it to go away only for something else to take its place or for the same thought to return.

For something that I found to be such a pain in the neck to do, I was taught various techniques to keep my mind focused on the task at hand, meditation. The main one was to focus on my breathing. I breathed in and out through my nose and sometimes out through my mouth, taking deep breaths each time. Listening to my inhalation and exhalation was soothing, but this technique eventually stopped working for me. My mind started to wander again. Then, I was taught to focus on the words "in" and "out" as I breathed in and out. Alas, I also got bored of that very quickly and my mind wandered aimlessly yet again. Perhaps incorporating both of these techniques together would make a difference. I inhaled and thought, "in" and exhaled and thought, "out." These two words would appear in my mind's eye as I breathed, and this worked momentarily. Then it was back to square one.

After two, maybe three failed techniques, I learnt a few more. "Try focusing on the expansion and contraction of your stomach," said my Reiki Master at the time.

When I did this, I seemed to also incorporate the initial two techniques that stopped working for me. It was strange, but multitasking had a better effect on me than focusing on just one thing. I think fusing the first two techniques did nothing for me because they made me focus on essentially the same thing and I was not technically multitasking. Or at least, my body didn't think so. I don't know. The thing is, I did not think I was supposed to multitask during meditation. I had a strong feeling I was only supposed to use one technique at a time. By no means was I an expert in the field and still am no expert so maybe we *can* use multiple techniques simultaneously. All I know is multitasking helped me focus during my meditation. If anyone wants to corroborate with me, that would be great! If anyone wants to disagree with me, please feel free to do so as well. I enjoy learning and would love to hear your take on this!

Finally, I learned a technique that I liked and could hold on to for quite some time. This was a visualization technique that I absolutely loved! It involved visualizing a smaller version of myself sitting at the center of my heart. Oh, I could do this very well. My mind was allowed to run wild and my imagination was being put to the test. Every time I meditated, I focused on my mini-me sitting in my heart center. It worked for a long time and it became easy for me to meditate that way. My mind would wander, but I was able to bring the focus back to my mini-me. I took into account what my physical appearance was prior to closing my eyes. For example, really looking at myself, the clothes I wore, my hairstyle that day, the way I was seated, you get the idea. I would then envision this version of myself sitting inside the center of my heart. Now there was a point of focus for me. It didn't matter that my mind was not blank. It mattered that I had a focal point, and that was very important to me. Even when my mind wandered, I would bring it back to wander on my mini-me instead. I focused on looking at the color of my clothes, the way my hair was tied or let loose, anything else that the mini version of myself looked like in the center of my heart that day. That was all that I focused on. If my mind wandered and I couldn't remember what I was wearing, I would open my eyes and take a quick peek at myself, then return my focus to my mini-me again. I was almost always able to remember what I wore that day because I made sure to look before getting into my meditative mode. If not, I would remember what I wore on a different day when I used this technique to meditate. Slowly, I was able to concentrate and focus my mind on that tiny version of myself sitting silently, smiling, in my heart center.

Soon enough, I started meditating with music. It wasn't a guided meditation by any means, just the sounds of a waterfall and everything that had to do with being in a scenic, forested area, basically, the sounds of nature. This was when my meditations started getting very colorful and vivid. Some would even call it wild. I walked with Buddha, Krishna and Jesus, to name a few, and I would talk to them. They would walk alongside me, ask me how my day was and such. We had long conversations during this meditative journey. They had messages for me and would accompany me until we had accomplished whatever we needed to during however many meditation sessions it took. Then whoever I was with at the time would hand me off to the next guide or divinity who had the next message for me.

These meditations lasted for months! The first divinity I encountered unexpectedly was Buddha. As I walked alone in the forest enjoying the sights and sounds during my meditation, Buddha appeared to me. He wasn't someone I typically prayed to, but I had started to read about him and slowly began to follow his teachings when I was involved at the Reiki center in Singapore. The longest I could carry on this very visual meditation was an hour. To sit still for a whole hour might seem long and arduous, but when your mind was active and wandered like mine, these types of visual, vivid, vibrant and vivacious meditations kept me focused. When the hour was up, Buddha and I would end our conversation and carry on from where we left off the next day when I went back into it. To shed some light and keep this simple, once Buddha gave me all the messages I was meant to receive from him, he would hand me off to Krishna, who handed me off to Jesus, so on and so forth.

Unfortunately, I was never able to reach my end destination in this particular meditative process. I was able to see my end-point, which was the top of the mountains in front of me on this windy road in the forest, where a majestic, white Ganesha was awaiting my arrival, but I was never able to reach this destination. I was constantly sidetracked and many things kept interrupting me over time. Sad to say, I was unable to get back into the beautiful forest and resume my journey from where I had once left off. The last guide I talked to on this path was a lion. Of course, it has been over a decade now so there was no way I could possibly get back to this particular spot where I had left off because I have no recollection of what any of the conversations with anyone was about anymore!

Another meditation technique I very recently discovered was to close my eyes and listen to everything around me. Considering I have been the sort of person who could never sit still in silence or focus on one specific thing, focusing on multiple things using one specific sense – clairaudience – was probably the easiest method of meditation with my eyes closed. I was able to focus on all the sounds around me. The intention was to stretch my hearing. I could hear the crickets, the lawnmowers, the dogs barking throughout the neighborhood, cars, the shutting of doors, children screaming and laughing, the birds, the wind, the silence, and sometimes I could even hear the rustling of leaves outside. That was so much easier than sitting in silence, listening to my breathing and focusing on the rise and fall of my tummy! When I was in the moment long enough, I could even hear what would seem like celestial music. These musical pieces would be playing right in my ears and on many occasions, I have walked through my entire house in an attempt to locate the source of the sound but to no avail. Celestial musical pieces, folks! My meditative experience could not get any better than that!

I mentioned that meditation was always a pain in the neck for me earlier, didn't I? It was a pain because of all the rules that I had to abide by. Sit still, silence your mind, focus on the quietness, don't think of anything, et cetera. Those were some very painfully annoying rules to follow, especially for a rule breaker! For me, meditation was never about sitting still or silencing my mind. It still isn't today. I love connecting with nature. I love calling upon my higher self and talking to her. She is my sassy self amplified tenfold and is always a joy to connect with. I love walking barefooted in my yard on warm days. As a dancer, dancing is meditative for me. For others, knitting is a form of meditation. Meditation for me can be connecting to a divinity whilst doing a card reading and channeling whoever is on the card. Sometimes more than one divinity would want to give me messages, not even necessarily from a card reading.

Washing dishes can be meditative. Repeatedly doing the same task over and over again mindlessly is meditation. If you think about it, you are in the moment when you are washing dishes, so as much as it is a mindless task, you are mindful by being in the moment. Some people enjoy cleaning their house. As boring as chores may sound, it is truly meditative because your mind is neither thinking nor feeling. You are living in the moment. You are just being and living in the present moment. Reading a book can be meditative too. When I read, my imagination runs wild. It is escapism into different worlds for me. I get so engrossed in the story and end up losing track of time and space. Isn't that what meditation is supposed to do? I strongly believe that if you have an imaginative mind, you can meditate. Simple! To me, meditation is truly about being in the moment, so be in the moment when you take a deep breath while you are outside!

Let's play a game. Close your eyes and take a deep breath in through your nostrils. Let it out slowly through your mouth and continue breathing this way as you perform this exercise. Pretend you are at a waterfall. Listen to the sounds and see the sights. Take in everything that is around you. What do you feel? What do you see? Do you hear the birds chirping? Are there butterflies fluttering about? Is there a gentle breeze or a strong one? What do you smell or hear? Are the water droplets from the waterfall sprinkling on you? Does this make you feel at peace? Is it keeping you calm? What are you feeling right now? That is what meditation is to me! You can either choose to stay in this world or let your imagination run wild and escape from reality! I would take the latter over the former any day.

Astral traveling is a form of meditation too. Using astral traveling, I have traveled to the past, the future and to different realms to meet various beings! It is quite fascinating! Of course, when you meditate and/or astral travel, always call upon your entourage of bodyguards. These can be your spiritual guides, guardian angels, ancestors, fairy guides, Archangel Michael, your spirit animals, power animals, your favorite deity, Jesus, Kwan Yin, literally anyone. I have recently started calling in the fairies, fairy guides, dragons and mermaids or merpeople. They will always protect you! It is okay not to know their names. It took me a long time to even know I had a spirit guide and found out I knew him when we were both in Atlantis in a lifetime a very, very long time ago. I discovered this when we took our first astral trip together to visit Atlantis to resolve something from my past life that was still affecting me in this lifetime. I originally discovered the issue during an Akashic Records reading one day.

Spirit Guides

In many of my online courses, the emphasis on a spirit or spiritual guide was apparent. The teachings always said to connect with your spirit guides regularly and have normal conversations with them as you would have with your friends and family. This is not an alien concept to me because I have mentioned in earlier chapters that I had no issues conversing with the divinities my entire life. And that is where the kicker is. Due to the years of practice, my habit was constantly calling upon and talking to the gods and goddesses, with whom I already have a wonderful rapport with and in turn, forgetting to converse with my spirit guides. I mean, I call them to be with me and protect me daily during my three-hour-long meditations but never have I ever had genuine heart-to-heart chats with the one whom I met in Atlantis.

As I sit here and write about him, he tells me that he is watching over me and is always here for me, even if we don't have long conversations. In the meantime, he encourages you to find your spirit guides as well. It isn't the end of the world if you don't necessarily meet yours right this minute, but it is always nice to have someone to talk to whenever you need it. If you do want to meet your spirit guides or guardian angels, there are tons of guided meditations you can find that will help you with this. While I didn't use any guided meditations to meet mine, during one of my online courses, I sort of took a shortcut and said something along the lines of, "My dear spirit guide or spirit guides, I would love to know who you are and connect with you. Please show yourself to me," and mine showed up. A few lectures later, there was a guided meditation to meet my spirit guide. What do you know?

You can use this method to call upon any being of light that you wish to get in touch with. Simply substitute the words "spirit guide" with "Jesus" for instance. Once you have established a connection with them, it becomes effortless to call upon them and invite them to partake in your everyday life. I have had strong connections with numerous divinities and deities since I was a child, and therefore, can easily call upon them. You might have had special relationships with some of them as well and may have lost touch along the way. That does not mean you can no longer call on them because you most certainly can. Call upon them and invite them into your space. Talk to them like you used to and go from there. It is very easy to build relationships with the divinities. They are always around and awaiting your call. Here's a tip. Start with a very simple, "Hello," and see where it goes from there. If you don't try, you will never know. If you are having difficulty calling upon them or hearing or seeing them on your own, be sure to look for a guided meditation of some sort. There are so many out there and I would highly suggest finding one that resonates with you. Sometimes, you might hear them say something before you see them. We all have some senses that are stronger than others, so don't fret if you can't see anyone. Try to listen out for them instead!

Conversations with My Higher Self

Recently a friend and mentor whom I met through one of the Facebook groups I am in had a one-on-one session with me when I first reached out about something in the group. She taught me how to heal myself through meditation. What? Is that even possible? Instead of using actual healing modalities to heal, how can someone use meditation to heal himself or herself? That was most definitely a foreign concept to me. However, we can! I have witnessed it first-hand! It came back to me during my one-on-one session!

How many of you have ever called upon your higher selves to talk to them? I used to when I did Reiki for people. I would call on their inner children, their subconscious minds and their higher selves to see what these clients needed to help them heal. After those Reiki sessions, I would sit down and talk to my clients and tell them what their inner children, subconscious minds and higher selves wanted them to know. My clients would be surprised and were curious to know how I received all that information considering the people who were the closest to them did not even know about what I uncovered during those sessions. Your body knows what it needs to help you heal, and so does your soul. The saying "your body is a temple" is not just about what you put into it or how you treat it. It is also about how you feel daily. If you're an angry person like me, then you are feeding your body with angry thoughts and possibly hatred towards numerous people and issues. Internally, we all require some sort of healing. Merely putting my hands on my body to heal alone wasn't enough anymore and for me to get to the next level in my spiritual journey, I needed to not only heal, but I had to release and let go of past issues that were still holding me back today. My husband always tells me something when he sees that I am starting to even remotely; get angry, "You do know that anger lowers your lifespan, right?" Wise words from this guy. Yes, I know, and I'm working on it. I usually thank him for pointing that out because I want to live a long, healthy and happy life! He might not believe in the type of work I do because he is a Science guy. He believes in reality and for me, my spirituality and reality are one and the same. I feel ghosts and he can't. So it is indeed my reality.

Just what exactly did this friend and mentor teach me, you ask? Well, for starters, she taught me how to connect with my higher self. Before we get into that, we first need to know what a higher self is. Everybody has a higher self. A higher self is the one who knows what is best for you as a person, what is best for your highest good and your deepest wellbeing in this current lifetime. This has nothing to do with the Akashic Records which we already addressed in several of the earlier chapters. They are not the same. Your higher self knows exactly what you are feeling, what you need at this time and at any time in your life. If you need sleep, your higher self will tell you. If you need to get your life together, your higher self will tell you. If you need to stop your alcohol addiction, your higher self will tell you. If you have mummy or daddy issues, your higher self will tell you. However, you must ask, and you better be ready for the answer! Sometimes, you might not even know you had these issues, so it is perfectly normal to be taken aback by what you discover. Ever since my own rediscovery, I started calling on my higher self and inner child to find out what I needed to heal.

Earlier, when I briefly mentioned my higher self, I described her as my sassy self amplified tenfold who is always a joy to connect with. My higher self looks like me and sounds like me. She is the fancier version of me because she makes an effort to dress up, do up her hair and loves looking good all the time. She is a fashionista on steroids. On the other hand, unless I have an event to attend, I am *very* comfortable in a pair of shorts and a t-shirt if

I am at home or a pair of jeans, a t-shirt and sneakers if I need to leave the house. My higher self tends to dress to the nines and appears to be clad in all the pretty dresses and high heels I own. At other times, she shows up in brand new outfits that I do not own, and that makes me think she wants me to go shopping. Hmmm. Strangely, she seems to love hats, something that I don't own or would ever wear. I keep telling her we aren't going for a costume party with big hats tilted to the side but she enjoys being fashionable and I will keep letting her entertain me. It is a win-win situation. I secretly believe she wants me to dress up and that's why she always appears to be looking the way she does. I will have to ponder over that but I still refuse to wear hats!

Not only does my higher self have excellent fashion sense (of course she does! She takes after me. After all, she mostly dons my wardrobe), her aura is also always effervescent. She usually appears to me with bright pink and green auras, heart chakra colors. It is usually her way of pointing out to me that I need to open up my heart more. Once we have said our initial pleasantries, I typically ask her what she would like me to know for the day and once she tells me, I go on about my day. By the way, in case any of you are wondering, this is part of my daily three-hour-long meditation process.

Coming to the point of healing through meditation, to take things a step further, I typically ask my higher self if she had anything, in particular, she wanted me to work on for the day. She usually did. This question can be one you choose to ask your higher self if you are unsure of where to begin. If you do know what you want to work on, you can say things like "take me to the time when I had my first heartbreak" or "take me to the first time I got angry." You can ask what sort of limiting beliefs you have. You can also ask, "Why do I have so much anger in me?" If you have a hard time getting along with someone, ask, "Why can't I get along with this person" or "what do I have against this person?" The answers you get might or might not be of surprise to you. Don't let the fear of the unknown prevent you from pursuing your journey of self-healing. You need to face these fears and only then will you be able to heal from within.

When I did my one-on-one session with my friend and mentor, I found out that I was affected by many incidents that occurred when I was at specific ages. If you are having trouble identifying specific events, try asking "at what age was I deeply affected by something that I am still having a hard time letting go of now" and see what numbers pop up. In my case, some of the numbers that popped up for me were four, seven, and twelve. All these numbers were very significant to me because I was always going through some kind of a transitional phase during these ages. At around the age of three and four, I entered nursery school, where I felt like I didn't belong. Around the age of six and seven, I was just starting primary school, another place that I felt like an outcast in. At the age of twelve and thirteen, I was beginning my secondary school journey where again; I was a pariah to my classmates and schoolmates.

At pretty much every stage in my life, I never felt like I belonged anywhere and this carried on my entire life. The only place I felt like I ever belonged was in my performing arts school. Everywhere else, I was a lost little lamb. I knew it, but because no one pointed it out to me, I was unable to let all of the pain and suffering go. I also didn't know how to let them all go. Once I was able to tap into those hidden memories that affected me at all those various ages, I was able to pinpoint specific events that caused me all that pain. My higher self went to visit the younger versions of me during those times in the meditative healing session. We (my higher self and I) asked my younger selves not to bother with what other people thought of me. My higher self said, "Look at me now! I am you all grown up and I am doing excellently! How many of the people who have hurt you can say that about themselves?" I honestly don't know how anyone else is doing but having said that, a smile appeared across the faces of my younger selves when these conversations took place. I knew we needed a confidence booster, something that I lacked in my younger days due to always being stereotyped and racially profiled. Some of the conversations were longer, while others were shorter, depending on how long it took to get through to my younger selves. These conversations definitely helped boost the confidence of my past versions. Who would have thought that with everything I have accomplished in my life today, all these things would still be haunting me to this day? They were so deep-rooted that I was carrying around so much hurt and baggage, unable to realize my full potential in both my personal life and my spiritual life.

That was such an eye-opener for me. Despite enduring so much emotional abuse my entire life in school, I turned out to be a strong-willed and psychically powerful woman. Hey, can I get an extra dosage of those qualities, please?

My higher self soon became someone I talked to daily. Of course, her flamboyance never ceased to enchant me. There were days that I also called in my inner child to ask her what she wanted me to learn or know about myself. I usually called her when I knew that I was lacking some playtime of my own. Invoking her was my way of reminding me to take some time out and do the things I loved. Unlike me, she had no problems telling me as it was. Usually, she appeared to me as my five-year-old version and would tell me, "Go play with your jigsaw puzzles," or "go watch a movie." In other words, I was supposed to do anything that made me happy as a child, that includes going to the playground and hogging the swing. Okay! I shall satisfy my inner child! Oh, wait! Wouldn't I be taking away an actual five-year-olds happiness by hogging the swing?

My Daily Practices

Remember when I said I spent about three hours daily meditating? You might think it is a lot. Frankly, I believe it is a lot too, but I could be exaggerating the length because I don't necessarily look at the clock before I start and after I have completed my daily ritual. It was always more of a go-with-the-flow type of situation. On some days, I have more to work on and on others, not as much.

My meditation routine is an amalgamation of a variety of techniques I learnt and picked up from various masters and teachers. The divinities also guided me to include extra steps to help me with what needed clearing or releasing. The routine starts with protection and grounding. This is a must for anyone who wants to meditate or even connect with your spiritual side. Grounding is crucial. You can attract all kinds of energies when you are in a meditative state of mind and may get psychic attacks. As a preventive measure and to keep yourself, your family, your pets and your entire property safe, *always* ground yourself and everyone on your property. I cannot stress this enough. Remember the portals in my house? If I didn't ground myself before meditating, I could have connected with the wrong beings. Therefore, please remember to always ground yourselves and protect your loved ones before you venture into your meditation.

What is grounding? It probably means different things to different people. To me, grounding means to connect to the universe's energy: connecting myself to Mother Earth and connecting to the source. It is the feeling of being protected by the universe. I like to envision the elements of the earth keeping me safe and sound.

A good example would be walking barefooted in your yard, on the grass and getting in touch with the way you feel in that present moment. Being present and mindful of what is beneath your feet, in between your toes, the wind against your skin and knowing that you are safe and protected.

Let me share with you a gist of my daily practices. This is not comprehensive because there are a lot of divinities and deities I work with that many of you might not be familiar with, so I am going to stick to the bare bones. You should typically have a quiet place where you can concentrate and be free of any distractions. If you are unable to find a quiet place, that is not a big deal at all. Put on your headphones, plug them into your electronic device and pull up some meditative music. It helps a lot. You can choose to sit in bed, in the living room, in a sacred space you have created for yourself specifically for this purpose, or outside in your yard. If the only place you have available is in your tiny bedroom closet, by all means, make yourself comfortable in there. Pull up a chair or sit on the floor; it doesn't matter. Just be comfortable in whatever space you have chosen for this moment. You will not receive any judgments from me! I have done it all. I would highly suggest a sitting stance instead of a lying-down-in-bed stance because I guarantee you will fall asleep. I've fallen asleep sitting, so imagine lying down.

When you have found your sacred or not so sacred space, get comfortable so you can begin. There are times that I chant "aum" or "om" seven times to increase the vibration in the space I am in before even starting the process but, I do not always do it. The difference in both chants is pronunciation and vibration. When you chant "aum," the pronunciation is "ah-ooo-mmm" and "om" is simply that. However, the vibrations felt in my body when chanting both of these are very different and therefore, depending on how I feel or want to feel, I decide on what word to chant. Should you choose to chant, know that you are helping to increase the vibration and creating a safer space for yourself? Imagine the sound of the chant moving up from your root chakra all the way through you to your crown chakra, opening all of them up as you repeat this seven times. You will feel the vibration within you. If you would prefer not to use headphones, then blast your meditation music wherever you are. I like listening to singing bowls, instrumental pieces, different types of chants, or sounds of nature. Anything that would help increase the vibration in your home will be beneficial. If you have a big house, feel free to let this music circulate throughout your home. You will feel so much energy when you do this. The piece of music you choose plays an important role in your ability to concentrate. Some chants allow me to focus better while others totally distract me. I prefer playing music without lyrics because I would be singing along otherwise.

Regardless of whether or not I chant, I call in Archangel Michael and his band of mercy to help clear the space and protect not just me but my family members who live with me and also my entire property itself. I visualize this white light filling the entire area covering everything within my property line. Every single protective measure I take and put into practice covers me, my loved ones – even if they are not within the property at the moment – including my pets, my house and my entire property. This is my mantra and I stick to it. Then, I envision the band of mercy gathering the beings who are in limbo in my space, my house, my property and taking them up into the light. Then there is a golden light that also protects us on top of the initial white light. So far, we have discussed two layers of protection. After that, I envision roots growing out from the soles of my feet downwards and wrapping around the core of the earth and I breathe in that energy. I visualize this energy coming up through the roots, up the soles of my feet, into my body, filling my entire being with the energy from the earth. This was a technique I learnt during my initial Reiki stages back when I was 18 or 19. At this point, if you are not already trying this with me, you should. Let's get some practice out of this, shall we?

There are some angels who protect each of the four corners or directions. Call them all in to protect you from the north, the south, the east and the west. What about above and below, you ask? Well, call in those angels too. This is the fourth layer of protection. You are protected from all directions now. Since I work with divinities from all religions, I tend to always call them as well. If you have specific deities or divinities you are more comfortable working with, call on them. You don't have to call the others that you don't work with or that you don't know. It might be more difficult for you to connect with them. Just know that you most certainly can choose to call them if you want to. When you do call them, start building your rapport with them. That way, every time you call on them, you can assure that your relationship gets better. It is the same concept as getting to know your spirit guides. The more you call upon them and interact with them, the stronger your bond becomes.

If you are close to Jesus and Mother Mary, call on them. In Chapter 13, I mentioned calling in your entourage of bodyguards. So call on your spirit guides, your guardian angels, your masters, and all the beings of love, light, compassion and wisdom, perhaps call on your ancestors and loved ones who have passed on as well. One thing I would like to point out here is that no matter who you call, they *will* come, and then some. Therefore, when you do call on all these wonderful beings to assist you with your protection and soon enough your meditations and whatnots, always emphasize that you are calling beings of light. For example, instead of saying,

"I call upon all of my loved ones who have passed on," say, "I call upon all of my loved ones who have passed on of light." By including the words "of light," it guarantees that only beings of light will come and be a part of this experience.

You do not want to invite anything else.

If I planned to work with a deck of cards today, I would call upon the folks who are on my cards as well. For instance, I decided to use my mermaid oracle deck today, I would say, "I call upon the mermaids or mer-people of light to be with me during this meditation and reading session," or at least something to that effect. Always add in "of light" to whomever you are inviting into your sacred space. After you have called in everyone you desire to be a part of today's session, call in your higher self and inner child should you wish to interact with them today. If you choose to call in your higher self or inner child, you can start asking them questions once they have made their appearance. Ask your higher self questions first, and then move on to your inner child, or vice versa. Don't confuse yourself and them by asking questions at the same time. If you decide not to call them in today, then go straight into whatever form of meditation you would like to start with. I typically begin manifesting all of my heart's desires first before going into other aspects.

I have added more oracle cards to my collection now and I love playing with all of them. Therefore, once I have completed my manifestations, talked to my higher self and inner child, I do card readings. Occasionally I pick one card from each deck for a combined reading. Otherwise, the norm is for me to work with each deck individually and do a one-card pull. What I ask is very simple, "What do I need to know today" or "what message do you have for me today?" I pick the card and channel the messages that I receive.

Sometimes I set aside the card readings until the end of the entire session because I want to have more playtime with them. I also do a karmic release for myself to help clear all the karma from all of my different past lives and present life. You can find tons of guided karmic release meditations online as you would a guided meditation to meet your spirit guides. The Internet is no longer a luxury product and Google is my best friend; so is YouTube! With the help of the divinities, I have also found ways to improvise karmic releases to make them my own and still keep the integrity of each karmic release session. However, for beginners, definitely find a guided one online, as these will walk you through each stage step-by-step.

When I started to practice reading my Akashic Records while taking the courses, I wrote everything down in a notebook. Upon completion of the courses with two different instructors, I didn't want to lose touch. Hence, I also make it a point to open up my records to do a reading every now and then. I usually only ask one question. Of course, I ask as many as I want answers to, but if there were days that I didn't need answers to anything, I do skip it. At times, when I am in the midst of this meditative process, I can't think of questions, but as soon as something pops into my head, I note it down either on paper or on my phone.

I said that I keep a notebook to record all of my own Akashic Record readings. I mentioned before that all of my readings and the messages I receive are channeled messages. If I did not record them down in some way, by the time the readings were complete, I would have forgotten every word. Just imagine, if there are days that I struggle to remember a single word that appeared on a card that I pulled, how on earth would I be able to remember anything from an entire channeled reading? Yikes! Recording my readings also helps me to keep track of my progress. I have asked the same question multiple times across the last six months and have noticed that I have progressively gotten better and healed some old wounds. You can choose your preferred method of recording any of your readings. I like writing them out. You can do a voice memo if that works better for you. If you are not camera-shy, you can also record a video. Whatever works best for you; whatever makes you happy! That's what you should do. Find your happy medium. If you want to post your readings on YouTube or other forms of social media, go for it! Make sure you comply with what the divinities say, though. They might not think it is a good idea to post this on social media. If so, work with them to find an outlet to share your readings if you want to share them somewhere. If not, keep it to yourself! The aim is for you to keep track of your progress. One day, when you look back at your first reading from day one and compare it with today's reading, you might be surprised to see how far you have come.

That just about sums up my entire three-hour-long daily meditative process. Sheesh! Bare-bones my foot. That seemed like a lot and might be overwhelming for some of you. Trust me. If I were you reading this book for the first time and got to the part about meditating for three hours, I would think I was insane too! I will not ask you to attempt this. All the grounding and protection work alone can take me anywhere between twenty to thirty minutes. Sometimes, even more, depending on what I am doing. It is not a simple process. It is tedious and time-consuming but very much necessary. However, once I got the hang of it, it became a breeze. These sessions do not always last three hours. They can be shorter depending on what I decide to do. They can also last much longer because I might decide to do live readings for people on the Facebook groups that I am a part of. Why not? I am already fully grounded and have completed my stuff for the day. I love doing live readings! Not only does it allow me to practice, but it also helps me get into a much lighter and happier mood than I was already in.

Do a live reading; don't do a live reading; that is your choice. At the end of your meditations, manifestations, readings and whatnots, always give thanks to all the beings of light that came to assist you during these sessions. Do this for every session. If you have decided to do readings for other people, make sure you wash your hands and clear the space that you have used. If you are a Reiki practitioner, you can follow the Reiki steps for clearing space using the Cho Ku Rei symbol on every wall of the room you have used and also the surface that you used to do your readings. As an added measure, you can also smoke the place using smudge sticks like sage, incense sticks or palo santo. For those of you who aren't Reiki practitioners, you can do everything else that was mentioned in the "added measure" part. Feel free to use any other method that works for you as well. Make it your own

Find Your Own Groove

Now that you have gotten a gist (really? A gist?!) of how I do my daily meditations, you can pick and choose what method works for you. Do not stress if none of the techniques is working for you right now. If you are new to this, patience is key. I know, I know! The girl who said patience is not her best virtue is giving you advice, right? Hah! Well, go ahead and try a method. Stick to it and when you know for a fact that it is not working for you, move on to attempt the next one. Numerous trials and errors are what got me to where I am today. I have learnt from multiple human and non-human teachers. Take what you can, learn from it, develop it and make it your own! There is no one-size-fits-all in this line of work. What ended up working for me might not end up working for you. You might even end up finding your very own groove! That is the beauty of spirituality.

I know that this is not an easy thing to be involved in. I also know that it might not be something you even want to be a part of on such a regular basis. If you do decide to partake in this journey, I say take your time and enjoy the ride. Don't rush it and definitely don't give up thinking you are not making any progress! Do it with a family member or a close friend who shares similar interests as you do. It is more fun when you have someone else to push you and encourage you, like exercising, which essentially is what growing your spirituality is. You are exercising your senses by putting yourself through numerous trials and tribulations finally coming out a victor. I loved doing this with my mother and sister and I seriously miss doing this with them. They are still practicing together in Singapore while I am practicing by myself in the U.S. As I mentioned earlier, my husband is not interested in this at all. If you are anything like me, I would strongly suggest finding a person to go through this beautiful journey with you. Otherwise, you would lack motivation without a peer to encourage you. Don't end up losing touch like I did because it becomes a chore to find that passion again. It is truly a blessing that I was able to find some friends in the online Facebook communities who have constantly encouraged, motivated and inspired me to consistently grow and better myself. Today, I can say that the interactions within the groups and with my individual friends helped me tremendously to keep my interest piqued in my spiritual journey.

We all have gifts and abilities. Should we choose to embrace them, our spirituality can soar to great heights. We might also have identical abilities, but the way I choose to access or tap into my gifts might not be how you choose to work with yours. We might not even be able to tap into them the same way. For example, I channel, which means I can hear and feel everything I am being told psychically. You might not be able to channel messages, but maybe you can see them and sense whatever it is the divinities are showing you or telling you. I might be able to communicate with animals while you cannot but perhaps you can communicate with plants whereas I can't. We are all different, yet the same because we are one with the universe. When we begin realizing that we are a collective, it becomes much easier to understand how everything is connected. My friend and mentor said that we are all intuitive beings, which means we are all psychics. It just depends on how we choose to use our gifts.

There have been times that I had thought of giving up. There have been times I told the divinities that I didn't want my gifts anymore only to have them tell me that should I choose that route, they would grant me my wish.

Of course, I did not give up my abilities. Had I given them up, I wouldn't be able to share my experiences with you in this book. I said things in the heat of the moment because of my irritation with certain situations and my anger issues as you have read about earlier. I just needed time to cool off and as I've said, the divinities have always been very patient with me. They know for a fact that I would not want to give up reading or seeing auras, and now that I channel their messages to the tee, they know that there was no way I would ever want to lose that gift and so many others that they have bestowed upon me.

I love sharing my gifts with people and even with the deceased ones who still constantly find me because they have been lingering on earth waiting for people like you and me to help them go into the light. How could I ever think of even forsaking my gifts when they stayed with me through all of my numerous phases in life? This has been such a wild ride and I don't want it to stop! I know that there is so much more awaiting me as I try to figure out the next step to move forward in my spiritual life. Right now, I am at the peak of my sacred spiritual journey, more than I was in 2012 and 2013. I know that I will continue undergoing innumerable trials and tribulations. Thankfully, I am always guided, protected and loved by all the lovely beings that I work with on a daily basis.

I found my spirituality originally through Reiki. Then meditation came along. One wonderful way for us to live life is to be happy and do what makes us happy, even in meditation! So I say find your happy place through meditation! If your happy place is somewhere you can pull up a chair and sit with your bare feet touching the grass while you watch the birds flitter and the butterflies flutter, then that is your meditation. If you choose to sit in silence, cross-legged on the floor with your palms facing upwards in your lap, chanting "om," then that is your meditation. If you are happy taking your dog for a walk and you both decide to stop and smell the roses, then that is your meditation. If you are happy traveling to different realms and lifetimes meeting new and old friends and acquaintances, then that is your meditation. You can either make all of these your happy places or none of these, and you end up finding your individual groove through various trials and errors. No matter what method you decide to embrace, you are the sole benefactor. Enjoy your spiritual journey because it is one of the most magnificent, life-changing experiences I have ever encountered. As I continue embarking on my journey, I hope from the bottom of my heart that it will be just as if not more awesome for you as well.

Conclusion

My spiritual journey has most certainly been a roller coaster ride! If not, it was undoubtedly a winding road with lots of hills and valleys. It has had a million highs and probably more than a million lows. All the setbacks I faced have indeed made me a much stronger person today than I was during the first seven years of what I thought was my spiritual peak.

I hope the meditative techniques in the book will be of help to you and your practice. Should you feel called to record the visualizations and replay them so you can be fully engulfed in the mindfulness practices, do it. I have many of mine recorded that I listen to all the time.

The road to rediscovering my spirituality has encouraged me to share my own sacred journey with you. 2021 would mark my 16th year since I started walking the spiritual path had I religiously soldiered on my spiritual journey without a break. But that's all right! What matters is I am now fully back into it and if I can do it after being lost for so long, so can you! If I have gone through something as drastic as totally losing touch with my spiritual side, wouldn't there be others like me out there too? Are you one of them, perhaps? Maybe you know of someone who is like that? Just like me, without having a support system, someone could have lost their way as well, wouldn't you agree?

You might not get your wake-up call through lower-dimensional portals in your house - I pray that won't happen to you – but you might get a wake-up call from a loved one who needs your help with something. Don't ignore it! It will keep gnawing at you until you do something about it, if not, there's always going to be an avalanche or a boulder that will either come falling or rolling your way! Trust me! I failed to heed my first twenty-million wake-up calls!

This book is here to let everyone who has fallen off the not-so-beaten path of spirituality know that it is okay to lose sight of everything, that it is okay to not know where you're headed. And it is unequivocally okay to feel lost and be lost. What you really need to know is that the divinities are watching over you as they have watched over me through these 16 years and my entire life even. Should you falter, they will guide you back to the path. Should you fall, they will catch you. Trust in them and trust in yourself! Know that you will get back on your feet and climb higher than you ever have!

No matter where you are in your spiritual practice, even if you have never gone through what I have, I hope you were able to grasp something from my sacred journey! It has been a sheer blessing to be able to share this with you. I wish you all the best in your very own sacred journey as well!

About the Author

Andrea Anne Aloysius is a financial accountant by profession. She was born and raised in Singapore and started to fully embrace her spirituality when she began practicing Reiki in 2006. She completed her first Reiki Master Level course in 2006 and again in 2020. She completed two online courses in reading the Akashic Records in 2021. Andrea has had extensive practice in meditation and mindfulness and works very closely with the Hindu and Ancient Egyptian divinities, among others. When she isn't working her full-time job at the financial institution, she does readings, healings and also coaches her clients on everything she has learnt. In her free time, she enjoys doing card readings for her friends and family. She frequently does various healings and readings for people in the Facebook communities she is a part of as a way of giving back. A foodie at heart, an animal lover, an avid reader and a total movie buff, Andrea is also passionate in all things dancing and performing. She would dance with anyone, anywhere! She loves traveling and two of her favorite destinations are Egypt and Clearwater Beach, Florida, she is an island girl, after all! Andrea lives with her husband, Marcus and dog, Fiona in Michigan, USA. Be sure to connect with her to be a part of all her adventures!

Connect with Andrea

Join her Facebook Group: Sacred Space – A Place For Sharing & Celebrating Little Wins In Life

https://www.facebook.com/groups/3082496735406504/

Subscribe to YouTube Channel: tripleaaacreations

https://www.youtube.com/channel/UCLmvQMaeRfHBhmKz9DurGqA

Follow her on Instagram: @a2thepowerof3

Services offered:

https://linktr.ee/andreaannealoysius

CPSIA information can be obtained
at www.ICGtesting.com
Printed in the USA
BVHW030800120922
646689BV00007B/21